T0221399

Politics Online

Politics Online

Blogs, Chatrooms, and Discussion Groups in American Democracy

Richard Davis

Routledge
Taylor & Francis Group

NEW YORK AND LONDON

Published in 2005 by Routledge
52 Vanderbilt Avenue, New York, NY 10017
2 Park Square, Milton Park, Abingdon Oxon OX14 4RN

Routledge is an imprint of Taylor & Francis Group, an informa business

© 2005 by Taylor & Francis Group, LLC

ISBN-13: 978-0-415-95193-7 (pbk)

All rights reserved. No part of this book may be reprinted or reproduced or utilised in any form or by any electronic, mechanical, or other means, now known or hereafter invented, including photocopying and recording, or in any information storage or retrieval system, without permission in writing from the publishers.

Notice:
Product or corporate names may be trademarks or registered trademarks, and are used only for identification and explanation without intent to infringe.

Library of Congress Cataloging-in-Publication Data

Davis, Richard, 1955-
    Politics online : blogs, chatrooms, and discussion groups in American democracy / Richard Davis.
       p. cm.
    Includes bibliographical references and index.
    ISBN 0-415-95192-5 (alk. paper) -- ISBN 0-415-95193-3 (pbk. : alk. paper)
    1. Political participation--Technological innovations--United States. 2. United States--Politics and government--Weblogs. 3. United States--Politics and government--Online chat groups. 4. United States--Politics and government--Electronic discussion groups. I. Title.

JK1764.D37 2005
320.973'0285'67--dc22   2004029781

Contents

Acknowledgments

Special thanks go to Stephanie Ord, who helped coordinate the completion of the research for this book. Others who assisted included Vincent James Strickler, Allison Gilmour, Robert Williamson, Amy Bice, Nicole Carlisle, Lindsay Baxter, Robert Floyd, Kristen Winmill, Linsey Sommers, Christy Watkins, Rachel Ballard, and Aaron Hassell. I am grateful to my family for tolerating my long hours away from home to write.

Introduction

▷ An April 1998 newsgroup post included the following statement: "CONFLICT START DATE: 19 APRIL ,1998. VALID TARGETS: ALL FEDERAL BUILDINGS." The announcement, along with similar posts, causes the FBI to issue an advisory on terrorism.[1]

▷ In 2001, a New Hampshire state legislator resigns after newsgroup messages he posted calling police "nothing but a bunch of vicious, brutal, crooked, racist, obnoxious, perjuring, bullying thugs" are publicized.[2]

▷ During the 2002 congressional elections, spam e-mail sent across the nation attacks a Georgia congressional candidate on her stance on terrorism and encourages voters to support her opponent. Such a practice is unknown before. The candidate loses her bid for reelection.[3]

Online political discussion forums such as newsgroups, chat rooms, e-mail, and blogs are a new force in American politics. The sheer volume of postings on the over fifty thousand newsgroups, seventy thousand public e-mail lists, thousands of blogs, and hundreds of chat rooms on any given day is overwhelming. Today, approximately 1.5 million messages are transmitted over Usenet newsgroups every day.[4] Internet discussion forums have suddenly developed into the subject of widespread public interest. They have become known as the new water coolers, where common people can air their gripes.[5]

The potential implications of this new tool for public discussion have not been lost on observers. One commentator suggested the opportunity to present ideas and information to millions now exists for people who might have been largely ignored before.[6] Online discussion has evoked paeans as a fantastic new mode of communication with the power to change the world of politics. According to Michael and Ronda Hauben, two early Internet advocates, the Internet's discussion component allows individuals to realize their power.[7] One such form, Usenet, has been termed the "public square of the Internet."[8] Indeed, like a public square, the breadth of discussion is mind-boggling—gardening, cancer, home businesses, opera, and on and on. There is also plenty of interest in politics as well. The scope of electronic discussion has spawned a joke about Usenet: not only is all human knowledge on Usenet, it is typed in every two weeks.

Public Embrace

Dramatic growth in participation in electronic discussion occurred during the late 1990s. According to the Pew Center, over a three-year period the percentage of Americans joining online discussions at least once a week grew from 23 percent to 35 percent.[9] By the end of 1997, estimates of participants in Usenet alone had exceeded two million.[10] This is about the same number of Americans who read *Cosmopolitan* magazine or *The Wall Street Journal.*

For many people, the interactive component of electronic discussion actually makes it more attractive than the World Wide Web. Communication with others is a major reason the Internet has acquired widespread acceptance. Internet users say e-mail is more indispensable to them than is the World Wide Web. E-mail is the most common reason people go online.[11] But it also includes participation in discussion groups.

The Internet has received the lion's share of attention from pundits, scholars, and journalists. But, due to its interactive capability, electronic discussion has attracted the attention of many Internet users. Today, more people log on to electronic discussion forums than read *The New York Times* or *The Washington Post.*

Democratic Corner

Moreover, electronic discussion's interactive function as applied to politics has earned it the label of the most democratic corner of the Internet—the province of the people rather than governmental institutions, associations, or companies. Since electronic discussion enables common people to express themselves politically to a potential audience of hundreds of thousands of others (and to do so instantly), it has been called "the people's lobby" and "our last, best chance to rekindle the great American dream."[12]

According to one advocate, computer discussion networks finally offer the reality of a direct democracy:

▷   In successful public debate, each participant is able to hear and be heard. . . . Democracy archetypes, the amphitheater of ancient Greece or the town meeting of colonial New England, offer appropriate metaphors. There is no comparable meeting place in democratizing nation states. Neither telephone discourse nor television dissemination provides adequate technological support. Computer networks alone successfully blend these capabilities into virtual town halls.[13]

Even public officials have been drawn to this new mode of communication with the public. The growing role of online discussion was demonstrated on November 8, 1999, when President Clinton became the first president to go online to answer e-mail queries from citizens. Presidential candidates in 2000 and again in 2004 went online for interaction with voters. Various news media organizations are using online discussion forums to disseminate news stories. Interest groups are utilizing online discussion as a mechanism for issuing press releases or other information about the group.

In contrast, there are those who have criticized online political discussion as at best trivial and at worst dangerous.[14] According to one writer, speaking of Usenet, "one of the chief applications of the Internet is not, it seems, so much to find out about things as to spout off about them."[15] Political discussion forums also have been found to be fraught with very unsavory behaviors, better known as flaming. Online discussions are often filled with caustic comments about others' views, and even personal comments.[16] Even without flaming, political group discussions tend to be dominated by certain ideological views, suggesting that the objective of such discussions is more reinforcement of opinions than a broad exchange of views.[17] Electronic discussion groups and lists have been accused of furthering extremists.

What This Book Is About

So what is this new form of electronic mass communication? Who are the people who participate? Is this the general public expressing its will on important public issues, or are these the rantings of a small minority of atypical people? Does this new medium offer the opportunity for common people to make decisions in a democracy? These are the questions that dominate this book.

The claims and criticisms about electronic political discussion have raised vital questions: Is this new forum an adequate means for expressing public will? Can we look to these networks as an accurate gauge of the public's agenda and will? Obviously, the answers impact the employment of electronic discussion as a tool for direct democracy or even just public deliberation on policy issues.

The major questions of this book are:

1. What is electronic discussion?
2. How does it function in politics?
3. How do participants in electronic discussion compare with the general public? Are they typical or atypical? If atypical, how are they unlike the general public?
4. Does electronic discussion possess the potential for usage as a tool for democratic governance, particularly as public space for political discussion and deliberation?

Before proceeding further, it is important to explain what this book is not. It is not a technical tome describing how Usenet, e-mail, or chat room technology works. Rather, it is specifically designed for those who know little or nothing about how computer networks operate. Nor is it a how-to book describing various electronic discussion groups of interest to surfers, particularly politically interested ones.

Simply, it addresses a fundamental question: does online political discussion possess the characteristics essential for political public space in a democracy? By understanding how electronic discussion works, who uses it, and how these people fill a representative function, we can answer that question here.

The first chapter explains why electronic discussion has become the subject of interest as a democratic forum, what electronic political discussion is, and how it has already effected change in American politics. The next chapter offers a description of the political world of electronic discussion, i.e., the groups, lists, blogs, and chat rooms discussing politics.

Then we turn to the people who inhabit these forums. Chapter 3 tells us about the posters—the individuals who carry the discussions in these groups. Who are they? What are their political attitudes? Next, in Chapter 4, we contrast the posters and the lurkers. Posters are individuals who express their opinions in these online forums, while lurkers are those who merely read. Are lurkers and posters alike, suggesting that the posters accurately represent the larger electronic discussion community, or are they substantially different, suggesting that forum content represents a vocal and atypical minority even within the online discussion community?

But can these online discussants be considered representative of the general public? In Chapter 5, we compare both posters and lurkers with the general public. How do those involved in electronic discussion differ from the general public? Are they similar to or different from the attitudes and behavior of the larger public? If similar, then electronic discussion could be a vehicle for gauging public opinion. This new platform could be a useful system for expressing and gauging public opinion in a democracy. On the other hand, if significant differences emerge between the online discussion community and the general public, then electronic discussion is not representative, and perhaps it is even dangerous to treat it as such.

Finally, we address the question of the place of online discussion in democratic governance. In Chapter 6, we describe ideal public space, contrast it with current online political discussion, and discuss what it means for the future.

CHAPTER 1

Electronic Political Discussion

On Nov. 2, 2004, long lines of voters greeted pollworkers in many states as the nation engaged in its quadrennial process of electing presidents. But the publicity over high voter turnout on that day masked the broader trend of decline in public participation in civic life. In most presidential elections since 1964 voter turnout has declined from the previous presidential election.

In 2000, just 51 percent of eligible voters participated in the presidential election.[1] In 1996, only 49 percent of eligible voters turned out. This number is the lowest since 1924. Voter participation also has declined dramatically for congressional and local elections.[2] In 2002, 39 percent of eligible voters participated in the midterm elections. By contrast, 47 percent turned out in similar congressional elections in 1962.[3]

The existence of a deeply rooted problem in the body politic has been visible in other ways. Public opinion surveys have shown widespread dissatisfaction with current American political institutions and processes. Levels of cynicism are high. The vast majority of Americans believe politicians do not care about them. The number of people who say they trust the government most of the time is nearly half of what it was thirty-five years ago.[4] Today, most people say they trust the federal government only some of the time or not at all.[5] In 1964, 29 percent of the public believed government was run only for a few big interests. By 2000, that figure had skyrocketed to 61 percent. And 56 percent of people believed that "public officials don't care what people think," compared with one-third who thought that way in 1964.[6]

The quarter-century shift in public trust, levels of cynicism, and feelings of political efficacy have worried many observers of the American political scene.[7] Following the precipitous decline in public trust in the 1970s, Seymour Martin Lipset and William Schneider claimed that "a crisis of legitimacy, a loss of faith" had occurred in the American political system.[8]

Recent political leaders have sought to tap this newfound cynicism to acquire electoral support. Former presidential candidate Ross Perot described American policy making as a system that "makes it difficult, if not impossible, to solve complex problems because it deals with images, sound bites, dirty tricks, fist fights on the floor of the house and things like that."[9] As a candidate, President George W. Bush talked of a "season of cynicism" and a "time of tarnished ideals."[10]

A variety of solutions have been proffered to rectify this problem of public cynicism and alienation. Some reformers point to the need for cultural change. Others advocate social or policy cures. Still others see a failure of organizational links and consider the reinvigoration of the parties to be essential.[11] Perhaps changes in news media coverage would improve participation, say other analysts.[12] Perhaps the blame lies with the public. Some point to the need for more civic education or the implementation of an obligation to perform civic service.[13] Still another set of reforms concentrates on the necessity of structural cures, such as a changed campaign finance system, more liberal voter registration requirements, or national initiatives.[14]

The Role of Communications Technology

Enhanced political communication may be a solution. Two analysts suggest the need for "the development of honest dialogue between leaders and followers in government, society, and the workplace."[15] For example, political talk certainly flourishes today via talk radio and television talk shows. Yet these "public spaces" may not be adequate for the task of reinvigorating public interest and enthusiasm.[16] Call-in radio is not thoughtful enough, while TV talk shows lead people to talk about the personal and intimate, but less so the political—particularly policy solutions.[17] The emphasis in these forums too often is expression, particularly shrill expression, rather than civil political talk.[18]

Increasingly, scholars, pundits, politicians, and journalists are turning to new communications technology to increase national political dialogue and reduce cynicism.[19] One scholar predicts that "the information technology revolution may . . . help government get closer to people, and when people feel a closer connection to government, confidence tends to be higher."[20] Another claims the Internet "will do by way of electronic pathways what cement roads were unable to do, namely, connect us rather than atomize us, put us at the controls of a 'vehicle' and yet not detach us from the rest of the world."[21]

One proposal rests on utilization of new electronic communications technology. Since electronic communications networks allow people to talk to one another and be heard by large numbers of others, they can certainly be used as a vehicle for political expression, deliberation, and perhaps even decision making.

Communications networks are seen as helping solve many of the nation's ills—such as alienation and societal disintegration—by facilitating political participation.[22] "[F]or all its problems, modern technology helps, more than it hinders, the promotion of democratic values and possibilities," argues Christa Daryl Slaton."[23] According to political scientist Anthony Corrado, communications networks hold the potential to "promote the type of interaction between voters and elected officials that is largely missing from modern politics."[24] Benjamin Barber predicts that "although it brings new kinds of risks, modern telecommunications technology can be developed as an instrument for democratic discourse at the regional and national level."[25] According to Barber, new technology can "strengthen civic education, guarantee equal access to information, and tie individuals and institutions into networks that will make real participatory discussion and debate possible across great distances."[26] A common view is that the future use of these networks will be the means for educating the electorate and perhaps closing the gap between politicians and the public.[27] There have been dissenting views arguing that new technologies, including communications technologies, may not further democracy, but these voices have been less audible.[28] A more common sense argument is similar to Douglas Schuler's that these electronic networks could lead to more democratic participation and less power by government and the corporate world or "increased government and corporate control."[29]

The emphasis of academics, good-government groups, and even politicians has been to determine how best to harness technology to transform the political system. In 1992, independent presidential candidate Ross Perot suggested creation of an electronic town meeting where people could discuss national issues. Meet-up technology, whereby people use the Internet to arrange physical meetings, was used extensively by presidential candidates, particularly Howard Dean, to mobilize voters in the 2004 presidential campaign.

As the Internet has grown in popularity, so has electronic discussion. Explicitly political discussion has grown as well. For example, the percentage of Internet users who participated in political discussions remained unchanged between 1995 and 1998, according to the Pew Center. However, since the percentage of Americans who are online users rose from 23 percent in 1995 to 41 percent in 1998, the number of electronic political discussion participants has soared dramatically during that period.[30]

The most common form of electronic discussion is e-mail. In fact, e-mail is the reason most people go online. But electronic discussion occurs through several formats, each of which has its own unique characteristics:[31]

Electronic Mailing Lists

A strong growth area in electronic discussion recently has been in electronic mailing lists or listservs. One Web site devoted to publicly accessible mailing lists estimates there are over seventy thousand such lists.[32] In addition, there are tens of thousands of others not publicly accessible.

Listservs are distinguishable from private mailing lists anyone can create. A listserv is a bulletin board where individuals post messages read by others. Others then post messages in response. The messages can be read only by those who are included on the mailing list. Again, this sounds like regular e-mail, but the difference is the presence of an intermediary, the list administrator or manager. Messages do not go out directly to the rest of the group. Instead, they are channeled through the administrator, who then sends them on.

An e-mail list is an exclusive medium because it is necessary to know about the existence of the list in order to subscribe, and also because the administrator has control over who is added, offering invitations to individuals to join the list or declining participation by others.[33] The administrator also controls what messages actually get posted. When an individual wants to post a message, he or she sends it to the list manager, who in turn disseminates the message to everyone on the list. However, the list manager can refuse to transmit a message. One electronic discussion analyst concluded that "most email lists operate as benign dictatorships sustained by the monopoly power that the list owner wields over the boundaries and content of their group."[34]

In actuality, the level of control a list manager exercises varies greatly. The distinctions between list types rest on whether the list is open or closed and moderated or unmoderated. Open lists allow anyone to subscribe, while closed lists screen participants. Moderated groups filter the posts, while unmoderated ones result in automatic posting once a message is sent. Open and unmoderated groups are the least controlled and the most public, while closed and moderated lists are more likely to maintain discussion focus and prevent postings by individuals outside a particular group.

Closed and moderated groups usually are not advertised publicly. Subscriptions are solicited from lists of individuals to organizations or associations or other lists of individuals the list owner wishes to invite to participate. One example of a highly exclusive closed and moderated group was a mailing list created by the British prime minister's office to engage academics, journalists, and Labour Party members of Parliament in a discussion of the party's "Third Way."[35] More typically, solicitations will be sent to networks of individuals such as specific policy experts or members of professional associations. One example is the following solicitation, placed on an academic mailing list:

▷ As you may know, I've been participating in a fairly low-volume distribution list of people who are interested in research *and* activism around the themes of democratic communication technology. The main point of this note is to ask you if you'd like to join. Although the details are on our (in-work) web site, I'll mention some of the main ideas in this note.

▷ We started the group nearly two years ago and now have about 35 participants from 14 countries on 4 continents. Our aims are to build a research + activism network that will be useful to its participants and to positively influence work in cyberspace and other communication arenas. . . .

▷ Each one of us is now asking other people if they would like to join. Our thought is that if we can get 100 or even 200 people, our network can be stronger, and more useful, both to us as researchers and activists and to the broader society. We hope that our work on this network will result in new journals and working projects, workshops and conferences, and other creative and influential collaborative enterprises.

▷ Help make this effort a success!

▷ Please let me know if we can add your name to our group.

Even when a group is closed and moderated, the degree of control still varies. Moderators take different stances. Some exercise a light touch, screening out only overtly commercial messages, spam, and other messages that are clearly irrelevant. However, others may be more heavy-handed in demanding that individuals stick to the topic under discussion.

Mailing List Topics

Mailing lists have proliferated, and today there are lists on a profusion of topics. For example, recreation is a popular topic for e-mail discussion groups. Motorcyclist groups discuss specific types of bikes or biking generally. A lifeguard discussion list is available, as is one dedicated specifically to want ads for swim team coaches.

Lists are devoted to specific baseball teams such as the Boston Red Sox or the Cleveland Indians. Some are even targeted to specific players. Sports card collectors trade actively on some discussion lists devoted to the hobby. Hunters can discuss their hunting dogs on another list. Some lists discuss specific recreation places, such as the Disney theme parks or hiking and camping in Utah.

Recreation is available, but so are more intellectual pursuits. Discussion of the works of philosophers such as John Dewey, René Descartes, and Confucius occurs on several lists. H-France emphasizes discourse on French history. Other lists converse on topics such as chemical engineering, poetry writing, and bee biology. Education is popular, particularly home education. Parents who home-school use e-mail lists to share ideas and information about the home schooling experience. Teachers of special-needs children interact on specific lists. Families who host international exchange students possess their own list.

A wide variety of vocations is represented on e-mail lists. Lawyers discuss a host of topics such as civil procedure, family law, and admiralty law, each of which has its own discussion list.[36] Scholars are joining lists to discuss specific research fields.[37] Historians of early America have H-SHEAR.[38] Ventriloquists discuss their talent on VentMail online. Professors have created discussion lists for courses.[39]

The objective of many lists is to offer a support group for participants. Daisy Girl Scout leaders discuss their troop problems on another list. Divorce Anonymous helps those who are going through a divorce. Spouses of police officers communicate online about their marriage experiences.

Some groups are designed not for discussion but for disseminating announcements such as electronic journals, travel advisories, or lottery numbers. Many groups are designed to foster social relationships, particularly romantic ones, by offering classified ads for single people.

E-mail lists are often tied into the World Wide Web through host sites. Some sites are portals for a wide variety of lists, while others feature a list or lists related to certain topics. The e-mail list can be subscribed to from the site. This applies both to lists created by organizations and to those accessed initially through their Web sites. For example, HIVlist and its accompanying Web site are designed to assist health care specialists who deal with AIDS patients.[40]

Drawbacks

Online discussion has its distinct drawbacks as a mode of communication. One obstacle is that the plethora of lists can be overwhelming. Finding a specific niche means browsing through a vast array of possibilities. Also, the "wild West" atmosphere of unmoderated, open lists can prevent coherent threads of discussion.

Still another potential problem is anonymity. Although sometimes touted as a virtue, identity concealment is easy to achieve through online aliases. According to Judith S. Donath, "One can have, some claim, as many electronic personae as one has time and energy to create."[41]

Incivility can occur. However, the existence of a moderator offers the opportunity for policing the behavior of individuals on the list. The list manager can take a more active role in threatening exclusion and actually expelling miscreants. Some lists even warn potential participants that they will be ejected from the list if they engage in flaming, or verbally attacking others.

Mailing lists are ephemeral. It is difficult to know when a particular list starts up or when it ceases to exist, since lists are so easy to initiate and close. One merely stops receiving e-mail messages. E-mail lists can die from lack of postings. Many mailing lists are functionally inactive since they are kept alive only by the list creator, who uses the list as a forum to express his or her views.

Usenet

Usenet differs in significant ways from e-mail. On Usenet, discussion occurs via newsgroups available through Web sites such as Google or through Internet access providers. These newsgroups do not actually provide "news" of the sort we might associate with the evening news or the morning paper. Rather, the content consists of typed postings by various individuals or groups.

Much like listservs, Usenet consists of bulletin boards where individuals can post their comments for all to see. This form of discussion has been termed a "many-to-many" form of asynchronous communication, in contrast to the one-to-many format of traditional media or the one-to-one of e-mail. *Asynchronous* means that individuals can respond at their own leisure. They are not communicating simultaneously, such as in a telephone call or face-to-face conversation. Rather, an individual can post a message on an electronic bulletin board and then wait for a reply. The wait may be in vain because no reply ever appears, or it may take minutes or days, much as when a message is posted on an office bulletin board with a specific request for action.

Usenet allows people to put up their comments for perusal by those who want to look at the messages posted for that particular topic. (Many posters will cross-post their messages, meaning they will post the same message to several boards simultaneously.)

Initially, newsgroups on Usenet were divided into three categories, each with a different name (*net, fa,* and *mod*). In 1985, that categorization was expanded to seven top-level hierarchies of groups: *comp, misc, news, rec, sci, soc,* and *talk.*[42] This small attempt at Internet structure was quickly met with opposition. A bevy of *alt* (or alternative) groups was formed to protest the existing system. The alt groups tend to feature discussion by more radical groups. Also, system administrators are more reluctant to carry them.

Today, hierarchical designations have exploded. Names now indicate countries, U.S. regions, U.S. states, localities, media organizations, colleges, and companies. For example, *biz* designates business groups and *bionet* biology-related discussion. Various countries were designated, such as *ca* (Canada), *uk* (United Kingdom), and *aus* (Australia). Other hierarchies identify localities, such as *tx* (Texas) or *ba* (San Francisco Bay area).[43]

Within these hierarchies, there are often more specific categories to designate particular topics of discussion. One example is *alt.current-events.clinton.whitewater,* the name of which denotes the group's current-events emphasis—a broad interest shared by several groups—but also this particular group's focus on Bill Clinton and, more specifically, the Whitewater scandal.

Usenet Growth

Usenet is an outgrowth of early Internet users' attempt to find a system that would serve as an alternative to e-mail. That system was a bulletin board process where messages could be posted to a central location and readers went to them, unlike e-mail, where the message came to the readers.[44] In 1979, a group of computer scientists at Duke University and the University of North Carolina found a way to transmit messages through a system of Unix computers. New versions of Usenet software were introduced in 1982, 1984, and 1987 to handle current and future increases in message traffic.[45] Growth was slow at first by current Internet standards. Interest in Usenet began small, with only three newsgroups existing in the first year and message traffic averaging only a few daily. By 1983, there were slightly over one hundred articles posted daily.[46] By 1996, there were over two hundred thousand daily posts on a total of approximately twenty-eight thousand newsgroups. By the end of 1997, an estimated two million subscribers were logged on.[47] In 1998, the number of groups was estimated to exceed fifty thousand.[48] The greatest impetus to Usenet growth was the creation of Deja News, an online site featuring Usenet newsgroups. The company claimed to have over four million subscribers to online newsgroups.[49] In February 2001, Deja News was acquired by Google. One indication of the size of Usenet is the fact that Google's database of seven years of Usenet messages includes approximately 650 million messages.[50]

Usenet as Community

Usenet has been viewed as more than a diverse collection of newsgroups. It has been termed an "electronic commons," "a regenerative and vibrant community," and even "a new social institution."[51] Sproull and Faraj portray newsgroups as virtual communities: "These electronic groups do much more than provide information. They offer the opportunity to make connections with other people. They provide support and a sense of community."[52]

Newsgroup communities obviously differ from those existing outside of the Internet world. These virtual communities are "not defined by many of the boundaries that sociologists and others traditionally have used to define communities, especially geography and political boundaries."[53] Proponents point to the discovery by many users of people who share their interests but with whom they never would have communicated without Usenet.[54] Stories abound about how the online communities form a support network for its for those who participate.[55]

Some have seen the Internet, and particularly Usenet, as a vehicle for bringing together people by overcoming physical and even ideological boundaries between individuals.[56]

> ▷ Welcome to the 21st Century. You are a Netizen (a Net Citizen) and you exist as a citizen of the world thanks to the global connectivity that the Net makes possible. You consider everyone as your compatriot. Virtually, you live next door to every other single Netizen in the world. Geographical separation is replaced by existence in the same virtual space.[57]

Gratifications

Attending to Usenet discussions is a time-consuming activity. One scholar wonders how people can spend so much of their time online. For example, if Usenet participants were to look at ten groups daily, each with fifty posts, they would be reading the equivalent of a two-hundred-page book. "How many people have the time or inclination to wade through that much text each and every day?"[58]

What do people get out of it? Obviously, some gratification occurs. Actually, several gratifications have been hypothesized. Many people seem to use newsgroups to meet other people with common interests. One survey found that 60 percent of Usenet participants said they had formed a personal relationship with someone else because of newsgroup contact. Over one-third even continued the relationship in other ways, such as telephone conversations or face-to-face meetings.[59] Usenet, then, appears to serve some "ordinary, even mundane, social uses" such as forging relationships.[60]

Also, it gives many people an outlet to discuss traumatic current events. Usenet can offer a forum for catharsis—discussing the impact on one's life of a sudden, unexpected event. Newsgroups brimmed with reaction to the World Trade Center attack on September 11, 2001, or the deadlock in the 2000 presidential election. As another example, within seventy-two hours of Princess Diana's death in August 1997, over forty-eight hundred Usenet postings had been made about her.[61]

Nancy Beym argues that Usenet groups offer individuals the opportunity to talk about issues relevant to their lives. She studied a soap opera newsgroup and found that the group discussion ranged far beyond the actual content of the programs and into other larger issues raised by the shows. Women who posted on the group were able to discuss issues such as sexual abuse and wife beating. Moreover, they were able to do so without the potential opprobrium of those in physical proximity to them, such as family, neighbors, or coworkers.[62] This raises the question of whether people are more willing to pour out their souls to perfect strangers who they will probably never meet personally rather than those with whom they have frequent physical contact.

According to Judith S. Donath, motivations to participate in online discussions, may include a desire to seek information or merely an interest in finding a forum in which to advocate certain positions. Still another motivation may simply be attention. Referring to people who discuss online groups, Donath suggests that, "as in the real world, their motivations may be complex: both the desire to be helpful and the desire to be noticed may prompt the writing of a lengthy exposition."[63]

Discussion on Usenet offers a controlled environment where interaction is predictable. Even though such discussion is widely public and entails surveillance by others one cannot even see or will never know, many people choose the loss of privacy in order to participate in the electronic environment. Participants are able to get communication pleasure but avoid potential communication pain.[64] According to Gary Gumpert and Susan Drucker, "Americans willingly give up privacy in exchange for safety, retreating into private worlds devoid of duty but filled with controlled contact."[65]

But is Usenet discussion a substitute for the activity the group discusses? Not really. Beym argues that the primary goal of the group she studied was "to enhance the pleasure of soap opera involvement."[66]

The Dark Side

Is Usenet creating community where none existed, or is it actually a poor substitute for real community? One argument is that rather than being a real community, electronic discussion is only the illusion of one.[67] The fear is these online forums have become a substitute for real community. A *Newsweek* columnist argued that the online chat room grief over the death of John F. Kennedy Jr. in August 1999 was "ineffably hollow—almost vulgar" because people online did not really know Kennedy.[68] It was virtual grief, not real grief.

Online community may at times actually displace real-world community. One Usenet participant who moved to a new city admitted, "I didn't know my new neighbors . . . but I knew who my cyberspace neighbors were."[69] Another, speaking of his cyberspace neighbors, wrote after two months online: "I know some of these people better than some of my oldest and best friends."[70]

Stephen G. Jones suggests that communication that occurs over computer networks is not much different from what occurs offline because we bring our personal traits to the Internet. In fact, rather than breaking down hierarchies, according to Jones, the Internet creates new ones—information elites whose presence has widened the gap between the haves and the have-nots.[71]

Another danger is online addiction. People are devoting increasing amounts of time to virtual communication with strangers rather than real communication with family and friends. Reports circulate of individuals becoming hooked through spending hours browsing Web sites or reading and posting messages on Usenet groups. People complain that Internet use has captured their spouses. Some students reportedly spend hours in front of computer terminals, miss classes, and flunk out of school. One physician described it as "a silent addiction that sort of creeps into your home. It's just a computer and it seems so harmless."[72] But proponents of online interaction argue that these fears are unfounded. Bill Gates, chairman of Microsoft, argues that newsgroups will mimic and supplement, not supplant, existing local communities.[73]

Usenet, like the rest of the Internet, has been criticized for its seamy side. Pornography is a common feature on Usenet, as it has been on the

Internet and other new media.[75] Usenet sex groups are estimated to average more than double the number of readers of other newsgroups.[76] Another fear, spawned by the anonymity of Usenet, is the potential for fraud. Without knowing whom one is talking to, it is possible to be lured into deceptive investment schemes or other financial transactions.[77]

Usenet, particularly, has been accused of harboring extremist ideologies and even fostering violent behavior.[78] The Internet and newsgroups have been blamed for providing an effective means of communication for violent groups and even helping disseminate practical information such as bomb-making instructions.[79] As a result, Congress passed legislation making such transmission over the Internet a crime.[80]

Newsgroup discussion often borders on the explosive. America Online (AOL) temporarily closed down a site based in Ireland for a "cooling-off" period because AOL administrators feared the intensity of the verbally violent clashes on the site.[81] In a more benign sense, Usenet is often portrayed as a haven for kooks.[82] Such a stereotype is reinforced by group titles such as alt.usenet.kooks, alt.religion.wicca, or alt.conspiracy.

The Breadth of Human Existence

However, Usenet is far more than pornographic discussions, hate groups, or "kooks." Usenet groups range widely in their subject areas. They essentially cover the breadth of human existence. Naturally, business has found uses for Usenet. Mutual fund investing is discussed in Usenet groups such as misc.invest.mutual-funds. As stated above, individual companies are initiating their own Usenet groups. Job seekers are posting their resumes on Usenet, while employers post job listings.[83] Some newsgroups, such as alt.forsale and the even more specific misc.forsale.computers.monitors, are specifically devoted to buying and selling between individuals.

Consumerism has acquired a voice in online discussion as well. Misc.consumers is a forum for people to share horror stories about companies or gain information about products and services. Some consumers are employing Usenet groups to complain about unfair corporate treatment or to check on consumer complaints before doing business with various corporations. Some Usenet groups have become public consumer complaint bulletin boards, as demonstrated in the Intel Pentium chip case.[84]

Usenet groups have become online book clubs. For example, Stephen King's books are analyzed on alt.books.stephen-king, while the literature of Appalachia is the subject of alt.appalachian.literature.

Talk of hobbies dominates many groups. These include board games (rec.games.board), photography (rec.photo.misc), or cruise travel (rec.travel.cruises). For outdoors enthusiasts, there are a wide number of groups discussing outdoor sports and hobbies. Discussions on how to design, build, and repair boats occur on rec.boats.building, while rec.gardens.roses features tips on growing roses.

Entertainment also attracts widespread interest. Opera lovers can frequent rec.music.opera, while country western fans favor rec.music.country.western. Fans of well-known entertainers form their own groups, such as alt.fan.hanson or alt.fan.woodyallen. Television show groups are popular, such as alt.tv.x-files, alt.tv.simpsons, and rec.arts.startrek.fandom, the last of which offers *Star Trek* fans the latest news related to the series and its spin-offs. Another category of entertainment groups attracts movie lovers, who can find groups about directors, such as alt.movies.spielberg, or those about genres, such as alt.movies.silent.

Humor is one of the more popular Usenet topics. On rec.humor, participants trade jokes and share addresses for Web sites of joke lists. Many posts on these sites refer users to an individual's Web site, suggesting that even many individuals employ Usenet to attract attention to their other activities on the Web.

Some groups unite fans of famous persons. These include alt.elvis.king, alt.fan.david-bowie, and even alt.fan.bill-gates. The group rec.music.beatles offers discussion about the history of the Beatles as well as current activities of the two living Beatles.

Sports talk is popular on Usenet. Baseball enthusiasts gravitate to rec.sports.baseball, where they can discuss team stats and trade rumors. Hockey fans discuss their favorite teams on groups such as alt.sports.hockey.nhl.vanc-canucks or alt.sports.hockey.nhl.wash-capitals.

Religious groups abound. Christianity, Islam, Baha'i, and atheism are discussed on a variety of groups such as alt.religion.christianity, alt.religion.islam, talk.religion.bahai, and alt.atheism. The topics can range more broadly on groups such as alt.religion, alt.religion.apathy, or talk.religion.misc.

Parenting, weightlifting, evangelical Christianity—nearly any imaginable topic either is the subject of an existing newsgroup or, given the ease in setting up one, may soon be. Not surprisingly, a common topic is the Internet itself. Groups discuss new hardware and software programs, hackers, spamming, Internet regulations, and Internet humor.

Usenet sometimes becomes a swift means of information dissemination as one participant asks a question, while another (often more than one) offers an answer. The following exchange from the rec.outdoors.fishing.fly.tying group provides an example:

> ▷ I don't fish much for trout, and I was just wondering, how many
>   of you fish for smallmouth bass and what is your favorite fly for
>   catching the "gamest fish that swims"?

▷ I fish for smallies quite a bit after June. Dahlberg Divers on top and Koch's Lampreys on the bottom. A Koch's Lamprey is a lead eyed bunny leech with a band of red dubbing behind the eyes that supposedly imitates the gills of the brook lamprey, a small lamprey native to midwestern streams. I also use a lot of wooly buggers and some clousers.

▷ George, you live up in Merrill right? I've never heard of these lampreys in the streams around here. Got any URLs leading to info on these? How about that "Koch's Lamprey"?

▷ Black/grizzly wooly buggers and chartreuse/white clousers work best for me. (I just tied up some clousers with bead chain eyes, trying to make a few lighter than the lead standard which sink too quick in shallow water.) A few odd nymphs also work.

Demographic groups proliferate on the Net. Ethnicity, race, religion, gender, even left-handedness—all find their niche in Usenet. Hispanics, African Americans, Pakistanis, feminists, veterans, Scientologists, Mormons, and many other groups are present on a variety of Usenet groups.

The Problems

Usenet discussion may sound idyllic as a forum for anyone to discuss anything. However, many of the problems with mailing lists also exist with newsgroups. There are so many subjects and so many groups that one criticism of Usenet is its increasing specialization and fragmentation. Though it may appear that every possible topic has been adopted by some group, Usenet actually grows because groups increasingly narrow their focus of discussion. Many groups grow from the more general, such as rec.gardens, to the more specific, such as rec.gardens.orchids; another example is from soc.genealogy to soc.genealogy.slavic, soc.genealogy.jewish, and soc. genealogy.west-indies. One commentator has called Usenet "narrowcasting in the extreme."[85] New software has appeared to help users find specialized discussion in the midst of the plethora of groups.[86] The predicted consequence is an increasing narrowing of interests and interactions. Users' exposure will be toward more homogeneity—people with interests and opinions much like their own.[87]

Usenet also has been accused of suffering serious deficiencies as an exchange medium. These deficiencies include information overload, too little moderation of discussion, anonymity, and incivility.[88]

Information Overload Since many political groups exist on Usenet, and discussion threads (the initial message and related responses) move quickly, participants can feel overwhelmed by the options for acquiring information and registering opinions. According to a Pew Center survey, 28 percent of Internet users feel overwhelmed by the amount of available information.[89] Usenet alone, with thousands of simultaneous discussions and millions of available threads, can be daunting. As one scholar has noted, "Even the financially and technologically quasi-elite who have access to the network do not in fact have a formal means to be present or represented in all matters in which they may feel interested."[90]

The growing usage of software designed to filter groups and messages and create a more customized Usenet presentation may address some of the problems with information overload.[91]

Too Little Moderation of Discussion   The vastness of Usenet, coupled with the posting of tens of thousands (potentially hundreds of thousands) of messages daily, has prompted criticism that this unstructured medium sorely needs organization. According to one commentator, Usenet "abounds with the superfluous, innocuous and mundane."[92] However, others give Usenet a less benign appraisal. One critic has criticized the Net as "cacophony rather than wisdom, a form of expression that follows not parliamentary principles but the Hobbesian law of the boring dinner party: it belongs, that is, to the person who talks loudest, logs on most often."[93] Another critic calls it a "Byzantine amalgamation of fragmented, isolating, solipsistic enclaves of interest based on a collectivity of assent."[94]

Unmoderated discussions allow many people to participate who may know little about the subject but like to talk. One scientist throws up his hands in despair: "You get professionals, interested amateurs, completely uninformed passersby, and schizophrenic street people all talking at once."[95] As a result, professionals such as researchers go elsewhere to carry on more specialized conversations. Many private organizations and research groups are turning to listservs because of their more exclusive nature.

Anonymity   Historically, citizen discussion in American politics has eschewed anonymity. Public comment and testimony to governmental bodies, public hearings, and town meetings all feature individuals clearly identifying themselves. This is not necessarily true in electronic political discussion. Since posters are often widely distributed geographically (and rarely, if ever, actually meet personally), Usenet political discussion allows a high degree of anonymity. It is increasingly difficult to identify a regional location, much less a specific physical address, for an individual. An address such as marysmith@aol.com offers little identification with a particular individual. Even that level of anonymity is not sufficient for some users. They seek even more secrecy by using unidentifiable e-mail addresses such as superspy@worldnet.att.net or the even more enigmatic 8up@001cu812.

Web anonymity may lead to an absence of accountability for one's statements. Therefore, individuals may express ideas they do not want to be responsible for. Or they may be less civil toward other participants because those others seem more like words on a screen than real individuals.

Interestingly, many discussion participants attempt to compensate for the blindness of online discussion. The normal nonverbal cues that we take for granted in interpersonal conversation—gender, age, race, height, weight, and so on—are absent in these interactions. Posters attempt to elicit personal information about others. Frequently they will ask questions of each other: "Where are you?" "What do you do for a living?" "Are you male or female?" "How old are you?"—in order to acquire data missing in text-based interaction.

Incivility   Incivility is a common feature of Usenet political discussion.[96] One journalist declared that "the Net is full of ranters standing on invisible soapboxes, and a great many exchanges essentially come down to: Enough about you. Let's hear from me."[97] Flaming is common in Usenet, especially in online political discussion.

Chat

A third online discussion forum is appropriately named "chat." It differs from mailing lists and Usenet because it is real-time, rather than bulletin board format.[98] Chat is held in various "chat rooms" or "channels," where the discussion among a small group revolves around a set topic. Everyone who goes to the room can read the messages and participate simultaneously.

In a chat room, participants type messages that can be immediately responded to. The message appears on the screen almost instantly. Other people will respond much like they would in a conversation where all are present in the room. Because chat goes on in real time, it is the closest to a real conversation of the forums discussed here.

Other similarities with traditional conversations exist. Chat rooms often include many people who merely follow the conversation—lurkers—without actually saying anything. Some chat rooms require a sign-in that allows all the participants to realize some people are merely lurking.

Also, some chat room participants sometimes will move their discussion elsewhere by alerting others that they are switching to another chat room. Some agree to meet in particular chat rooms and specific times in order to have a conversation. They also can create private chat rooms where they invite only certain individuals and exclude everyone else.

General chat channels exist where anyone can join in the discussion. Internet Relay Chat is the largest noncommercial system of chat. However, much of chat, and particularly chat engaged in by less sophisticated Internet users, exists via Internet portals established by familiar offline organizations. America Online, for example, offers its own smaller and more exclusive chat areas, also organized by topic.

Software allows individuals to limit their chat to those they want to talk to, such as those on AOL members' Buddy Lists.[99] Like Usenet and listserv, there are chat rooms for every taste, encompassing hobbies, recreation, travel, politics, and more. Some Web sites sponsor chats where famous people, such as Dr. Ruth Westheimer or John Madden, are available for an hour to take questions from fans. Celebrity chats with famous authors, entertainers, and sports figures have become common on sites such as Yahoo, CNN, or the Microsoft Network. Investors use chat rooms to exchange stock news and debate the wisdom of various investments.[100]

Chat channels are owned by someone who establishes the channel. This is true not only for the portals, as discussed above, but also for those who establish chat channels on Internet Relay Chat. The chat channel owner can control who enters the chat channel and whether they get to stay there. Some chat channels, particularly those administered by various commercial portals, are moderated, particularly when they are sponsored by existing organizations and feature a guest. Chat channels occasionally feature particular discussion topics at set times, such as health at 2 P.M. or the economy at 11 A.M.

Chat traffic is not as heavy as Usenet or e-mail lists. One estimate suggested at least 170,000 users talk daily on nearly 40,000 channels.[101] However, chat participation ebbs and flows depending on events individuals want to discuss, such as the outcome of a highly publicized trial, the outcome of an election, or the sudden death of a celebrity.

Chat, like Usenet and e-mail, does not necessarily stay online. Some chat discussions do lead to relationships outside the chat room.[102] But such activity concerns many parents, who fear that online chat rooms may become havens for pedophiles seeking victims. *U.S. News and World Report*, referring to online discussions such as chat, opined that "the Internet is a perfect breeding ground for victims looking to be victimized."[103] An FBI operation found that twenty-two of twenty-three "children" on a decoy chat channel ostensibly designed for children actually were adults seeking sexual contact with children.[104]

Drawbacks

For those who want to mimic real interpersonal conversations, chat comes closest. Yet there are drawbacks. The nonverbal cues are still missing, as they are in Usenet and listservs. As a result, chat rooms also can devolve into incivility due to the lack of a human face and the inability to convey nuances and subtleties such as sarcasm.

Another drawback is the superficiality of the discussion level on chat. This occurs because the message space is brief (usually no more than a line or two allowed at any one time) in order to keep the conversation going rapidly. Messages fly onto the screen very quickly. If an individual attempts to type a lengthy statement, the conversation probably will have passed on to another subject before they finish writing it. Such superficiality does not pose a difficulty for light social conversation. However, more intensive conversation, particularly about policy, becomes difficult to sustain in a chat room environment.

The rapidity of the conversation requires quick reading and rapid response in order to participate effectively in the discourse. Those who do not pay attention may find that the conversational thread has already shifted elsewhere. The advantage rests with those who can type quickly. One chat guide explains that "you don't shout louder than everyone else to be heard . . . ; instead, you type faster than everyone else."[105]

Perhaps unlike real conversations, chat room discussions talk over one another. Several conversational threads exist simultaneously, and it often becomes necessary to ignore some of the threads in order to follow one. Joining a conversation, abruptly in the middle, also may border on rudeness elsewhere. Though waiting to see what the conversation is and seeking to join it, many chat participants enter the room and often merely throw out a statement or question in the middle of a thread, hoping to change the topic or at least add another thread.

Moreover, unlike listserv and Usenet, the messages are ephemeral. Once they scroll off the screen, they disappear. There is no record of chat as there is for Usenet and listserv. One cannot return to a prior statement. On Usenet, it is possible to review the thread in order to determine what has been said before. E-mail messages can be saved in order to chart the course of the conversation. But chat lacks that memory.

Anonymity seems to be preserved in chat, as it is in other discussion forums. However, unlike Usenet or listserv, it is possible to know who is joining in the conversation and who is leaving. As a result, it is possible to know who is just lurking. But anonymity is not absolute. Many chat rooms require people to register to participate, thus providing the chat room sponsor with identifiable information. And a participant may encourage specific individuals to "talk" instead of stay in the background.

However, the identity of individuals can be cloaked by aliases similar to those used in Usenet. Even though some chat rooms require registration, the individual can create a screen name that may or may not be his or her real name.

Blogs

The latest form of online discussion is the Web log, more commonly known as the blog. Started in 1999 with the dissemination of software allowing people to create their own Web logs, blogs are similar to newsgroups since they consist of postings by participants. But blog content is much like that of a diary or journal entry. Organized in reverse chronological order, many blogs evoke a strong intimacy as bloggers pour out their secrets to anyone who wishes to read them. Blogs are the written form of home videocams, where people live parts of their lives in front of cameras broadcasting to any person who happens on their Web site.

Blogging is less like an actual conversation and more like people reading in each other's Journals. Yet dialogue does exist, as bloggers talk to each other through their blogs or post comments on others' blog entries. Bloggers form small communities in which members reference others' blogs in their own, suggesting a public conversation being carried on in a public square, but involving details of the lives of the people in the small blog community. In fact, linking is one of the measures of the popularity of a particular blog.

Although blogs have had some publicity in the traditional news media, the blog community is really a small niche. According to a 2003 survey by Ipsos-Reid, only 17 percent of Americans even knew what blogs are. Only 5 percent said they had ever read a blog, while just 1 percent of adults were regular blog readers (at least once a week).[106] Those who do blog are very young. More than half of all blogs are created by people under the age of twenty.[107]

Also, blogging appears to be a temporary phenomenon for many bloggers, according to a 2003 survey of the blog community by the Perseus Development Corporation. The survey of randomly selected blogs found that two-thirds had not been updated in two months, suggesting temporary or permanent abandonment. The survey found that one-fourth of blogs did not last more than one day.[108]

The most well known daily blogs, such as Blogger and Boing Boing, are rarities in the blog community. The Perseus survey found that the average blog is updated once every fourteen days. Fewer than one out of eight blogs is updated daily.[109]

Similarities and Differences

Each forum described in this chapter possesses distinct advantages. The newsgroups and blogs offer an advantage over the other two outlets in that they are the most public of all the forums, while listservs often are the most exclusive. And compared with chat, which is based on brief real-time discussion, newsgroups and blogs allow political discussion to be more substantive. Listservs may focus the discussion more by excluding participants outside a certain offline association or group and by limiting the messages allowed to be posted. In the real-time talk of chat, individuals who participate need not wait for another participant to log on and respond; they can engage in a dialogue similar to one conducted interpersonally offline.

The choice of format may reflect the desires of the participants. Those seeking a more exclusive, more controlled, and focused discussion may gravitate to mailing lists, particularly closed and moderated ones. Those who want more immediate discussion and are not interested in expressing lengthy thoughts may find chat rooms more to their taste. Those who like freewheeling, more public forums with greater opportunity to write lengthier and perhaps more substantive posts are most likely to seek a newsgroup or a blog for public expression.

Electronic Political Discussion

Is there a political role for these forums? Does this online discussion make any difference in political processes, institutions, or mass attitudes or behavior? Such a role certainly has been widely predicted. The Internet has been touted as a medium for empowering common citizens to unite to gain political power. Al Gore predicted the Internet would "promote the functioning of democracy by greatly enhancing the participation of citizens in decision making."[110] It has been termed a "powerful technology for grassroots democracy" and one that, by "facilitating discussion and collective action by citizens, strengthens democracy."[111] Online discussion itself has been called "the most democratizing aspect of the Internet" because through it "citizens will gain new opportunities for participation and a voice in politics, governance, and society."[112]

Direct Democracy

The most wide-reaching role predicted is as a social force actually displacing existing representative institutions. The result will be a new governmental structure based on direct citizen governance. No other invention has possessed more potential for implementing direct democracy than the

Internet. The electronic forums for discussion on the Internet offer the promise for citizen participation, public expression of views on current policy matters, and even the prospect of online voting.

Electronic discussion has been offered as a forum for the construction of direct democracy because it apparently possesses essential characteristics for such a role. One such trait is equality. Discussion online offers the potential for democratic interaction because, as one author puts it, "practically every single individual on the Net today is available to every other person on the Net."[113]

Another is the opportunity to freely express views in online forums. According to Hauben and Hauben, the potential for allocating power to individuals via the Net cannot be overstated:

▷ For the people of the world, the Net provides a powerful means for peaceful assembly. Peaceful assembly allows people to take control of their lives, rather than that control being in the hands of others. . . . Any medium or tool that helps people hold or gain power is something special that has to be protected.[114]

The vision is of a tool to bring people together, virtually, to debate and determine public policy. Through electronic political discussion, we have been promised a new "conversational democracy" where "citizens and political leaders interact in new and exciting ways," and individual citizens will be able to "communicate directly with other citizens locally or throughout the nation."[115] Others have suggested that the Internet and electronic discussion "present the chance to overcome the obstacles preventing the implementation of direct democracy."[116] Electronic discussion is the ultimate democratic forum, it is claimed, because people can participate when it is convenient to them, they can have time to be thoughtful, and, once again, everyone gets to participate.[117]

Current Obstacles

Yet this vision of a new democratic structure mediated by electronic political discussion forums is not here yet. Nor is it likely to arrive until a few significant obstacles have been overcome. The first obvious barrier is that direct democracy is not necessarily a desired goal in a political system structured to avoid such an outcome. But laying aside that concern for the moment, let's examine other barriers.

One is inequality in levels of accessibility. Electronic communication has spread quickly among the well-to-do but is largely inaccessible to the have-nots.[118] For example, according to the U.S. Department of

Commerce, while four out of five households making more than $75,000 a year are online, less than a third of households making under $25,000 annually have Internet access.[119] As a consequence of this online economic divide, some fear that the Internet—and its discussion arms—too easily can become the haven of the affluent and eventually the middle class, but effectively bar others from access.[120] As Langdon Winner has put it, "People equipped with personal computers, modems, cellular phones, and the like have begun to outshout those in our society for whom owning a telephone may conflict with paying the rent or the doctor."[121]

Without universal access across society, electronic discussion is less useful as a political tool. Hauben and Hauben claim that "until free or very low cost access is universally available, the Net will fall short of its potential."[122] As a result, many advocates of the expansion of Internet access have called on the federal government to play an activist role in funding.[123] Benjamin R. Barber contends the government has "a fundamental responsibility to assure the American public and its civil-society institutions free and equal access and usage."[124] The Clinton administration set a goal that "every classroom, library, hospital, and clinic in the United States must be connected to the National Information Infrastructure by the end of the century."[125] Legislation has attempted to make Internet access universal by reducing telephone rates and assisting schools and libraries in acquiring Internet access.[126] The governmental initiative prompted a large-scale shift in classroom access. By 2001, 99 percent of schools had Internet access.[127]

However, government role disturbs some who believe the Internet's autonomy from government will be compromised. Even some of those who express concern about access disparities argue that the problem is solving itself as the costs for hardware and online access fall.[128] Bill Gates contends the Internet will not cost individuals more than they spend on other services such as video rentals, newspaper subscriptions, long-distance telephone service, and so on because all of these will be available online.[129]

Another barrier is the fragmented nature of electronic political discussion. The online discussion forums today lack the mass-medium component of, say, television in its early days, where only three or four channels existed and consumers had few options. As a result, political television attracted large audiences. In the 1960s, the vast majority of American households watched political conventions or presidential speeches.

However, today's political discussion competes with discussion on a plethora of other topics. Many people may be on electronic discussion forums simultaneously, but they are virtually in thousands of different places, most of which may be unrelated to politics. Even if the groups they visited were political, that does not mean they would be speaking to each other, since political groups are numerous and disparate.

Deliberative Democracy

However, direct democracy is not the only possible outcome of Internet discussion. Another scenario, one less radical by comparison, is utilization of the Internet's discussion colloquia as a facilitator of public delibera- tion.[130] Deliberative democracy has become a popular term for informing the electorate before encouraging participation. A number of advocates of deliberative democracy such as Benjamin R. Barber, James S. Fishkin, and David Mathews have become vocal in recent years.[131]

Several experiments with deliberative democracy, at both the national and local levels, have been conducted as well. One experiment conducted by the Jefferson Center for New Democratic Processes in Minnesota selected electoral juries—groups of citizens—who deliberated and made public recommendations. Another was James S. Fishkin's National Issues conventions, where average citizens participated in a national convention designed to deliberate on current policy issues.[132] This new medium offered a public sphere in which citizens could interact with each other and deliberate about policies.[133] "If properly applied," one study contends, "new communications technologies can nurture deliberation and help citizens educate themselves into democratic decision-making."[134]

Yet there is a realization that there are serious impediments to even this role, much less direct democracy.[135] The most formidable barrier is human—the tendency of society to rely on technology to solve problems. New technologies cannot solve problems; only people can.[136]

The potential of electronic discussion networks for direct democracy strikes fear in the hearts of many observers of politics. One fear is that policy will be "based on little more than emotions" created by dramatic stories and images.[137] The outcome could be anarchy: "Power to the people could mean that nobody is in control, with unpredictable political consequence."[138]

Another possible unwanted outcome is that individual citizens may not be able to cope with their new online civic responsibilities. Howard Fine- man put the question this way: "What if our presidents become nothing more than the sum of our whims and misinformation? The netizens of the future will have to take their jobs seriously. Are we ready for this much democracy? Let's hope so."[139] Advocates of electronic political discussion as the new forum for direct democracy, such as Michael Hauben and Ronda Hauben, counter citizens can perform such roles: "Usenet news- groups and mailing lists prove that citizens can do their daily jobs and still participate within their daily schedules in discussions that interest them."[140]

Current Role of Electronic Discussion

Electronic discussion has already begun to play a role in American politics, albeit far more limited than direct democracy. With millions of people following electronic discussions, and occasionally posting as well, political topics obviously are acquiring broader interest and participation. In addition to its role as a vehicle for online political expression, electronic political discussions also have offline repercussions for American politics. It is those repercussions that give the hundreds of thousands of participants a clout far beyond their numbers. Electronic political discussions sometimes affect the agendas both of the public and of policy makers. This sometimes occurs directly through public officials' observation of and reaction to Usenet discussion threads. But more frequently the medium is the journalistic community.

Media Usage

Electronic political discussion forums have been predicted to possess the potential to replace the news media. They have been termed "the perfect antidote to modern mass media" because their content is provided by many instead of a few.[141] According to Hauben and Hauben, "More and more people on Usenet have announced their discontent with the traditional one-way media, often leading to their refusal to seriously read newspapers again."[142] If true, that would constitute a major shift from citizen information gathering via established journalistic organizations to reliance on the online postings of average citizens or other organizations outside traditional media. Some advocates are claiming that electronic political discussion is restructuring the concept of news as "people begin to realize that they can provide the news about the environment they live in and . . . this information proves worthwhile to others."[143]

Instead of displacement, however, news media organizations are beginning to utilize these forums for their own purposes. Discussion lists and newsgroups are becoming new journalistic information sources. The American Press Institute tool box for reporters contains a directory of mailing lists for journalists to consult.[144] Newsgroups are becoming popular sources for journalists to follow specialized topic discussions.[145] According to one survey, 43 percent of journalists said they browse through newsgroups. Of those who browsed, nearly half said they did so at least weekly.[146] Journalists also solicit information from newsgroups by following group discussion and then posting messages seeking information, including interviews, for stories. One journalist posted a message asking for help in covering the epidemic of mad cow disease. The journalist received a variety of messages in return, including notice of the existence of a previously unknown mad cow home page.[147]

Journalists are using discussion groups and mailing lists not only to gain access to expert sources but also to measure public reaction. On September 11, 2001, journalists turned to Internet discussion to get news. A *Washington Post* reporter used a private listserv to obtain "the human contact to match the rush of news." The reporter took the following comment from an eyewitness to the World Trade Center attack writing on the listserv: "It's a beautiful late summer morning, and as the sun hits the towers, you can see the glass glinting as it falls, like confetti, blown out by the heat of the fires."[148]

But another purpose of tracking online discussion on 9/11 was to gauge public reaction to the events of the day. A *New York Times* reporter related that "the feelings expressed on the Web ran the gamut from intense anger—'I'm going to find out who did it and kill them,' wrote one poster to CitizenX.com, a Web discussion site—to deep sadness. On many of the Internet discussion groups, participants blamed Arab terrorists for the acts, and anti-Arab sentiment and slurs abounded."[149] Some reporters even used online discussion to measure public reaction internationally.[150] One online discussion forum, Minnesota E-Democracy states that one of its purposes is to offer "the media unique insight into the public's reaction on the news."[151]

The uses can be policy-oriented as well. For example, one reporter seeking reaction to anti-gay legislation sought it on a gay and lesbian chat room.[152] Archiving software available through the Google search engine means the effort of tracking online discussion about an individual, organization, or issue has become easier. Journalists also join mailing lists on topics related to their own beats, such as science, environment, or the economy. By following such lists, they can keep track of developments in various fields.

There are risks, however. Since Usenet is a public forum, posting requests for sources in a newsgroup can alert competitors to a news organization's story interests well before publication occurs. As a result, journalists could be scooped while still in the process of gathering information.[153]

Not only do journalists use these online sources for news gathering, but the news media have become the object of discussion in some groups. Journalists and others discuss media practices in newsgroups such as alt.journalism, alt.journalism.print, and alt.journalism.criticism.

News media organizations are using announce e-mail lists to push news onto subscribers on a regular basis. Customers can receive specialized news bulletins, based on their own particular interests, via e-mail. News organizations also are incorporating electronic discussion forums into their Web sites in order to increase Web site usership. On www.nytimes.com, Web visitors are invited to post messages in political discussion groups focused on topics such as the Middle East, drug policy, or the death penalty, in addition to groups on many other topics such as finance, travel, or entertainment. News organizations such as the *Washington Post* and CNN allow site users to chat with others about the news of the day. Some news organizations feature guest experts or politicians who chat with site visitors for an hour online. The *Washington Post* sponsors chat rooms with different guests throughout the day. *The Christian Science Monitor* site features "e-Monitor conferences" where participants can discuss a variety of topics such as genetic engineering and intellectual property rights.

Interaction with Political Actors

Political actors—from the president to various interest groups to the news media—have found online discussion a new mode of political communication. It is less important for the actual interaction, particularly at the national level, when so few citizens can actually pose questions or make comments. But it does offer an image of the politician as technologically current and interested in interacting with ordinary citizens.

It was in 2000 that campaigns began to take the Internet seriously. Online discussion also played a role in campaign embrace of the Internet. Presidential campaigns aggressively used e-mail announce lists to reinforce and mobilize their own activists. Al Gore's campaign home page encouraged visitors to become online field organizers responsible for sending e-mail to their friends. Republican candidate Steve Forbes appealed to supporters to sign up their friends on Forbes' e-mail distribution list. Forbes' supporters were urged to create an "e-block" with as few as twelve other people. When an individual subscribed five thousand people, he or she became a member of Forbes' "National E-Committee."

But the campaigns also used other forums in addition to e-mail. Some presidential campaigns tried to alert politically interested Internet users to the site's existence by posting messages on Usenet groups. They monitored online discussion to see how the candidate was being portrayed in these groups. Then they urged activists to squelch negative rumors and issue supportive messages for the campaign.

Candidates also appeared in online chat rooms. John McCain's campaign made the senator available for an online chat session sponsored by the campaign, but it required those who actually posed questions to the candidate to make a financial donation to the campaign. A regular feature on the Gore site was the town hall format, where Gore would answer voters' questions posed to him. However, the campaign controlled which questions were asked.[154] The Gore campaign introduced a new online reinforcement mechanism in which Gore supporters were encouraged to sign on to a campaign-sponsored online chat room where they could discuss the campaign with each other.

Presidential candidates have not been the only users of electronic discussion for campaigning. Candidates for local or state races use newsgroups to advertise their campaigns. The most useful venue is the local or state politics group or list. But some candidates with potential national support appeal for broader nonconstituent involvement in their campaigns. One Republican candidate who called himself a "pro-life, pro-Second Amendment, Catholic, fiscal conservative" made a plea for group subscribers to visit his Web site in order to help him in his campaign.

The 2004 presidential campaign accelerated the use of online discussion. As early as January 2004, 4 percent of Internet users said they were participating "in online discussions, blogs or 'chat' groups about the elections."[155] One of the most significant developments in 2004 was the use of meet-ups, where a candidate's supporters could arrange a time and place to meet locally. The meet-up concept was designed to assist Internet users who shared similar interests to make physical contact with each other in their own communities. The Dean campaign pioneered the adoption of meet-ups by a presidential campaign, but other Democratic presidential candidates promptly followed. By the time Dean withdrew from the presidential race, over 160,000 people had signed up for Dean meet-ups. The Dean campaign was not the only one to attract supporters to meet-ups. The other campaigns quickly realized the organizing potential of this technology for electoral campaigning. By the time John Kerry had won enough delegates to secure the Democratic presidential nomination, 78,000 people had signed up for his campaign's meet-ups.[156]

Another innovation was the use of campaign blogs. Candidates or their staff posted blogs on the candidate's Web site announcing news and documenting the candidate's activities and reactions. As with nonpolitical blogs, the tone was first-person and familiar. Candidate staff usually posted blog messages. But candidates and/or their spouses occasionally posted on the campaign blog. Elizabeth Edwards, wife of Senator John Edwards, was a frequent poster on her husband's campaign blog.

The use of blogs differed among the candidates during the 2004 presidential election. While the Democratic presidential primary candidates considered blogs to be open forums where dissenters were allowed to present their views, the Bush campaign blog was used as an opportunity for supporters to hear from campaign leaders. The open approach meant many blog entries were posted by opponents of the candidates. For example, on February 24, the Kerry campaign posted the following comment from a reader on its official blog: "I've seen more independent thought coming from my dog than from the democrats I've read on this blog."

In addition, campaigns encouraged visitors to the campaign Web site (or subscribers to the campaign's e-mail lists) to establish their own supporter e-mail lists (or adopt preexisting ones) to further dissemination of the campaign's messages. This approach allowed the campaign message to reach voters whose e-mail addresses were not available to the campaign. According to John Hlinko, General Wesley Clark's director of Internet strategy, "We made a very conscious decision that we wanted the Web site to not be just a brochure, but a tool that supporters could use to evangelize for us."[157]

Meet-ups, blogs, and supporter e-mail lists—2004 innovations—all were designed to use electronic discussion to serve campaign goals of identifying potential supporters, reinforcing those who had decided to support the candidate, and transforming passive supporters into active advocates for the campaign.[158] The Dean campaign's early acceptance of these technological tools spurred speculation that the Internet would make Howard Dean the Democratic presidential nominee in 2004. Dean's loss undermined such speculation. Clearly, the jury is still out on how successful these tools are and whether that success ultimately affects electoral outcomes.

Citizen-Government Relations

Public officials also are using electronic discussion as a means for signaling their interest in citizen input. Elected officials are using chat rooms to answer questions from discussion participants concerning policy and politics. For example, congressional Republicans used chat to gain support for their patients' bill of rights legislation.[159] However, the democratic nature of chat in asking questions of politicians is illusory. There is still a filter in the sense that over the course of an hour (the usual time limit for politician involvement) very few questions can be asked and very few participants can ask questions compared with the large number observing the chat.

Public officials also are creating blogs to permit a human side to show. This also allows the official to set his or her views out to constituents. A few state legislators are using blogs to inform their constituents of activity in the state legislature as well as to solicit comments and retetions from constituents. Oakland mayor Jerry Brown runs his own blog about Oakland and California politics.[160]

It is difficult to predict whether blogs will become as commonplace as websites for public officials.

Groups

Candidates and public officials are not alone in incorporation of electronic discussion forums into their persuasion campaigns. For example, many interest groups have their own specialized electronic mailing lists. The Audubon Society supports twenty-three lists on topics such as horseshoe crabs, birds in Mexico, and Texas butterflies.[161] But it is also incorporating Usenet groups and chat rooms into its mobilization strategies. Such groups instantly reach people who share the group's goals. The proliferation of Usenet groups and e-mail discussion lists with narrow, specialized interests aids lobbying groups in identifying and mobilizing supporters.

Newsgroups, it has been argued, also will play a part in this process of fomenting collective action.[162] Some movement has already occurred. For example, in 1989, a newsgroup—soc.culture.china—served as a communication and mobilization medium for Chinese students outside China during the Tiananmen Square democracy demonstration and the government's subsequent crackdown on dissidents.[163] Students used newsgroups and chat rooms to communicate during the revolt that brought down Indonesia's president, Suharto, in 1998. One analyst concluded the Internet did not alter the outcome, but "it fast-forwarded things."[164]

In the United States, groups also have energized some citizens via online discussion. By posting messages on a variety of newsgroups, the Taxpayer Assets Project, a public interest group, successfully killed a provision of the Paperwork Reduction Act that would have limited public access to government documents.[165]

Several specific benefits for groups accrue from their use of these forums. The group gains access to a list of activists subscribing to the newsgroup who also likely share the group's interests. The group can distribute information about the group's activities beyond its own membership. It can signal supporters to mobilize for or against pieces of legislation critical to the group's interests. Again, those informed and mobilized may not actually belong to the group but are sympathetic to its position.

E-mail lists also serve this purpose for groups. The group hopes individuals on its own e-mail distribution lists will take immediate action, when called to do so, by sending e-mail or fax messages to policy makers. This is especially true when the group actually embeds links to policy makers' e-mail addresses or Web sites in the message itself. But some groups also rely on existing networks of mailing lists to promulgate group-related information. For example, the ACLU disseminates online news through its ACLU Action Network, which posts messages about the group's activities on a range of sympathetic mailing lists. The post urges recipients to "take action today" on some issue of importance to the ACLU. The group's message includes its Web site address for more information.

Electronic Discussion as Opinion Gauge

Given the technological challenges of connecting everyone to the Internet, the vision of a direct democracy via the Internet is a long-term prospect even for the most ardent advocates. A more immediate usage of electronic political discussion is as a gauge for public opinion. This gauge concept has become increasingly accepted by those who measure public opinion, usually via the news media. Attention to electronic political discussion postings from the general public usually have stemmed from media coverage. Yet the journalistic practice of eavesdropping on electronic discussion groups is raising questions about exactly what journalists are reporting. Journalism scholar Tom Goldstein presents the dilemma: "You don't know whether this is a thin segment of the world, or it's a real issue [being discussed]."[166] Nevertheless, as mentioned earlier, the practice of using online groups or lists to measure quick public reaction to an event or issue is spreading.

Representation

Increasing usage of online discussion as a vehicle for persuasion and mobilization suggests that electronic forums are important in the formation and expression of public opinion. Yet the use of electronic talk as a public opinion gauge raises the question of representation. Can opinion expressed in online discussion forums be considered representative of public opinion? By what measures is this public opinion? Is the substance of this opinion reflective of more broadly based public opinion? Are those who speak online appropriately representative of the online population? Are they representative of the general citizenry?

These questions are critical because of the value of public opinion in a democratic society and the inherent complexity of adequately measuring such opinion. Even public opinion polling is a form of representation in the sense that those surveyed stand in for others who are not surveyed. Through scientific random sampling and objective questioning, the chosen few—typically between six hundred and twelve hundred adults—can accurately predict public sentiment in many cases.

A direct democracy, as advocated by some proponents (particularly using the Internet as the mechanism), seemingly negates the necessity of representation. Since no one stands in for anyone else and all participate in decision making, representation does not exist.

However, the U.S. Constitution was not written as a structure for direct democracy. The Framers created representative government partly because a direct democracy clearly was not feasible at the time. But they would have opposed the latter even if it had been practicably achievable. They feared the people's too-direct role in the process of governance. In "The Federalist No. 10," Madison argued that direct democracies "have ever been spectacles of turbulence and contention." He favored representative bodies that would filter popular will and produce a situation where "the public voice, pronounced by the representatives of the people, will be more consonant to the public good than if pronounced by the people themselves."[167] As a result, representatives—members of Congress, U.S. senators, the president—stand in for the citizenry.

Even direct democracy in practice is a representative forum. Athenian democracy included only a fraction of the residents of the city-state—those who were citizens and thus eligible to participate in decision making. In essence, those citizens stood in for all others who were affected by policy but viewed as unworthy of citizenship. Direct democracy in the United States, as represented in New England town governance—our modern version of direct democracy—features a model closer to direct democracy than Athens ever created. Any resident of a New England community using town meeting governance can participate by attending the meeting and voting on town policy. However, many do not. Those who do become, in a sense, the representatives of others.

Still, more direct democracy has become the norm in American politics, at least in theory. In many ways, elected officials have been given shorter and shorter leashes by the public. Increasingly, legislators have been expected to track and follow public mood swings and more accurately mirror the wishes of their constituency. This has occurred despite the fact that populations have increased in each district and state, which means members of Congress now represent nearly thirty times as many people as the first representatives did in 1789.

The democratization of policy making suggests that the public communicates more often with elected representatives and that representatives, in turn, are expected to gauge public opinion more frequently. As a result, the public's will is assessed constantly, and not just during electoral periods. Such public will may not be manifest in a decision-making process, but the policy maker must anticipate what the public's response might be if elements of the public became involved in the process.[168]

Because legislators know they can be punished for not reflecting the public's will, they constantly seek some measure of public opinion—something that stands for the public—in order to understand public opinion. According to Marie Collins Swabey, policy makers' inability to know what the public is thinking at any given time obliges them to "accept the expression of the will of a part of the people as a substitute, with the consequent chances of error and mistake."[169]

Public opinion surveys offer such a substitute for the public will. The sample becomes the representative of the general public, a broadly accepted practice because of the scientific nature of drawing the sample. However, such surveys are costly to administer and often are fraught with their own problems, such as loaded questions, assumption of respondent knowledge, or sampling bias.[170]

In fact, policy makers more often rely on less scientific methods of taking the public's pulse, such as correspondence from constituents, unscientific mail questionnaires, newspaper editorials, and conversations with constituency opinion leaders (prominent business leaders, local government officials, educational administrators, and so on). Although they are well aware of the self-selected nature of this sample, members typically lack other means for assessing opinion.[171] According to Harold Gosnell, "The representative, a good part of the time, fumbles in the dark so far as knowing his constituents' minds through external communication."[172]

Journalists now play a role in the feedback mechanism between legislators and constituents. Acting as a trustee of the public, reporters ask the questions the public is expected to ask or convey external reaction to public policy decisions. Yet journalists have been criticized as inadequate representatives given their own independent and sometimes conflicting imperatives of commercialism and peer acceptance within the journalistic community.

Deficiencies in existing methods have left policy makers seeking other manifestations of the public will. The preference is for a mechanism that is easily accessible, is instantaneous, and accurately reflects public will. Electronic discussion clearly offers some of those traits. It is easily accessible: policy makers (or more likely staff) can access discussion in seconds. It is inexpensive: little cost is expended beyond the costs of hardware and Internet connections, which are already provided to policy makers, and staff time to collect data is fairly minimal. Moreover, the feedback to policy actions is instantaneous: people respond immediately to events, sometimes within hours or even minutes of an event's occurrence.

The availability and ease of use of online discussion for gauging public opinion does not mean that policy makers have embraced this forum for such a purpose. That is not the point. Rather, it is that the potential for such usage, tentative at first, is present. And as policy makers perceive participants as probable voters, that usage likely will increase.

But if policy makers increasingly turn to this type of forum as one method for taking the public's pulse, a critical question remains: is this the public speaking? Some signs would suggest so. As discussed earlier, online discussion involves many people. With hundreds of thousands (and potentially millions) of participants, electronic discussion appears broadly participatory. Moreover, it may be more representative than some other gauges policy makers use. Unlike the news media or constituency leader opinion, the content of online discussion does not overtly constitute the reaction of an identifiable elite. In addition, online discussion participants possess the aura of "just folks." They hold no formal leadership roles. They appear to be regular citizens armed with a computer and a modem or broadband connection. Further, journalists already have legitimated the representative role of online discussions by reporting electronic discussions in news coverage. Politicians who pay heed to online discussion content similarly prove that this role already exists.

On the other hand, do we know who these people really are? Are they typical of common citizens? Do their views represent those of the general public? Are they what they are often taken to be?

The first step in answering these questions is determining what representation really means. Two general views of representation have been suggested.[173] One concerns representation as doing, while the other approaches representation as the act of being.

The former perspective concentrates on the representative's activity. Does the representative's activity conform to what the constituency would do if they were in the same place? In that sense, the representative's voting behavior is a mirror of the constituency's will. Sometimes termed "the delegate," this representative must determine what the public's will is and then act in that manner. It is possible for the representative to so thoroughly reflect the constituency's attitudes that such a search for opinion is not necessary. The delegate view imagines a relatively egalitarian relationship between the constituency and the representative.[174]

There is a contrasting interpretation of representation: the representative as trustee of the public.[175] Rather than reflecting the public's opinions, the representative acts on behalf of the constituents in the legislative chamber. Representing the interests of a constituency means furthering those interests, even though they may conflict with the constituency's immediate wishes. This approach to representation suggests that the representative is wiser, more intelligent, and more devoted to a higher public good than are his or her constituents. That elitist view cannot be publicly advocated by politicians, nor can it be practiced in cases where the public's will is clearly stated. Yet ever since Edmund Burke proposed it in the eighteenth century, it has been a popular perception of how a representative should characterize his or her relationship with a constituency.

Still another form of representation, however, is based on the representative's act of being. The representative represents if he or she carries a descriptive likeness to the constituency. According to Hannah Pitkin, a representative body is characterized by "an accurate correspondence or resemblance of what it represents, by reflecting without distortion."[176] Using this approach, a truly representative body is a mirror of the demographic composition of the electorate. This concept of representation is present when voters expect their representatives to reflect their racial, religious, or economic backgrounds. It was the basis for the creation of majority-minority congressional districts, which, it was argued, were necessary to create a legislative assembly that mirrored the nation as a whole.

In this book, we will examine both types of representation. Does electronic discussion represent the public in terms of doing? Does the issue agenda of electronic discussion correspond to that of the general public? Are electronic discussion participants discussing the same kinds of issues as the majority of the public, and taking the same kinds of positions?

In applying this form of representation, it should be noted that there is no implication that these online participants consciously attempt to mirror the will of the larger public. Online discussion communities may obliquely refer to the general public, much as people do in face-to-face political discussion. However, there is no evidence they seek to adopt the role of representative of those not online or those who do not express their views online. This examination will only uncover whether such a correlation between public opinion and online discussant opinion actually exists due to the expression of the latter's individual views through this medium.

In terms of representation as being, the question arises: do electronic discussion participants demographically and attitudinally represent the general public? That is, are they like the general public not only in terms of demographic components, such as age, race, gender, income, and other characteristics, but also in terms of attitudes such as interest in politics, trust in government, political efficacy, and the like? The purpose of this book is to examine the state of online political discussion and then address this issue of representation by comparing and contrasting online discussion participants with each other and then with the general public. Finally, this book contrasts current electronic political talk with the characteristics of ideal public space and offers recommendations on how we can successfully move from the former to the latter.

But first we need to understand more about the world in which political electronic discussion exists and operates. Now we turn to that analysis.

CHAPTER 2

The Political World of Electronic Discussion

▷ I wouldn't put anything past this right winged bunch of dictatorial facists [*sic*]. If they wanted to bring his plane down, they could, very easily. The technology exists to disable a plane electronically, in mid flight. And that is what they probably did.

▷ Too many changes in the candidates on the Democratic side for comfort, Carnighan [*sic*], Torricelli, and now Wellstone. All were close races where the Democrats had a huge incentive to change the horse in mid-race. Torricelli backed down, Wellstone wouldn't. This smacks of a DNC hit. How did Ted Kennedy know not to be on that plane?

▷ Of course we are all shocked over Wellstone's death and are curious to know all the details. Anger is only a natural reaction to many who share in the grief of losing a great senator who devoted his entire life in the service of his country.

▷ My heart goes out to the friends and family members of all who were lost in this tragic accident.[1]

These newsgroup posts, written on October 26, 2002, the day after the plane crash that killed Senator Paul Wellstone of Minnesota, demonstrate the tone of threads on one newsgroup following a major news event. Political newsgroups become the forum for some people to express themselves immediately on current events, and often with great emotion. Such an event focuses attention on political figures and politics, even for those who are less interested in politics.

However, such notice is rare because political talk hardly dominates electronic discussion. The vast majority of discussion is nonpolitical.[2] Only nine of the top one hundred most-posted Usenet groups are about politics, and only two of the top one hundred most-read Usenet groups are explicitly political.[3] Obviously many more groups discuss issues that are political. But the use of the word *politics* is a cue to potential participants that the group has explicitly political discussions.

However, even if only a small fraction of these forums is dedicated to politics, that still encompasses hundreds of thousands of participants who are using electronic political discussion regularly. Some of them post, but many more just read others' posts.

Still, those who participate in political discussion groups appear to be more prolific as posters than those in nonpolitical or less politically oriented groups. For example, while the estimated average number of posts for all Usenet groups is slightly over 1,200 messages per month, American politics groups have an average of 2,870 messages per month.[4]

Political Diversity Online

But what exactly goes on in the political world of online talk? If it is not just extremists talking about making bombs, then what is it? Political life is as varied in the world of electronic discussion as it is in real life. In fact, it appears much more diverse than what most people normally would see in their own neighborhood. Ideologies and affiliations appear online that rarely surface in suburban or rural American life, and sometimes not even in many urban settings. One of the benefits of the Internet's presence, it could be argued, is the exposure an individual can have to new and varying opinions and political ideologies. Groups that do not fit in the mainstream—"fringe groups"—welcome the potential of the Internet to help them locate supporters and form a common bond.

But, as was pointed out in the last chapter, electronic discussion is not just the province of fringe groups and ideas. Taking each of the forums in turn—e-mail lists, Usenet, chat, and blogs—we can explore the range of forums and conversation topics extant on current political discussion.

Politics by E-Mail

Political e-mail lists deal with hundreds of diverse topics such as the environment, Marxism, or the Libertarian Party. The ease of forming a new list facilitates the fragmentation of mailing lists. Anyone can form a private list. Even creating a public list is not a difficult process. Hence, the world of political e-mail lists is one of many addressing highly specific themes.

Lists can be centered at particular levels—international, national, regional, or local. Many address primarily local political topics or political issues within a particular state. Mailing lists discuss local politics in places such as Ypsilanti, Michigan; Ontario, California; and Blaine County, Idaho. Some even specialize in specific state or local issues, such as a list that addresses Connecticut state taxes.

Announce lists or those emphasizing one-way communication from a central source, usually an organization, can be political tools for interest groups. Common Cause uses CauseNet to announce the organization's activities and solicit member action on policy issues. NARAL Pro-Choice America's Action Network keeps members informed on issues related to abortion policy.

Interest groups form lists to announce group activities or allow members to interact with each other through discussion. The lists also can be a vehicle for recruiting new members or at least publicizing the group's views to a wider audience. For example, JBS, the list of the John Birch Society, is designed to attract new members to the group.

The dramatic growth in the number of mailing lists may well be attributable to the usage of this new tool by specific organizations as a vehicle for collective action. Using mailing lists, groups can communicate with their members more immediately and at lower cost. Often these organizations will open organizational issues to discussion via the mailing lists. These lists are usually closed in order to keep the discussion internal. One example is the BakersfieldDems, a mailing list restricted to members of the Democratic Party in Bakersfield, California.

Mailing lists also are organized to support candidates for elective office. In the 2004 presidential campaign, lists emerged such as PresidentBush2004 and WesleyClark2004. But local lists also formed for various presidential candidates such as IowansforKucinich or ArizonaTeachersForDean. Other lists appear in order to express opposition to candidates. From 2004, examples include Dubyahs_Follies, BushMustGo, and UnelectGWBush. Nor are presidential campaigns the only subjects. CharlesWalkerForCongress supports a Georgia congressional candidate while Steinbrueck discusses a candidate for Seattle City Council.

Party organizations, as noted above, particularly at the state and local levels, have instituted lists for intraparty communication. These include not only the two major parties but also minor parties such as the Libertarian, U.S. Taxpayers, and Reform Parties. But even partisans have fragmented further. One example is the Gaylibertarian list, which appeals to libertarians who are also gay or lesbian.

Yet the vast majority are not tied to particular organizations but are the work of individuals who, according to the list descriptions they write, have a variety of motives. As stated above, anybody can form an exclusive or public list. Some individuals form lists in order to provide themselves with a forum to advertise their views. One e-mail list, 1GuysThoughts, is one example among many of an announce group set up by an individual who sends a regular message to subscribers describing his opinions on current events and issues. Others are attempting to attract like-minded individuals to activism, while still others appear to simply enjoy engaging in debate.

The issue topics of lists vary widely. The list Hate-crimes discusses the proliferation of hate crimes, while Racial-issues deals with racism. Gun control, capital punishment, and welfare reform are all list topics. Ideology is a popular topic in listserv creation. One list blatantly calls itself "a conservative slant on some current affairs." A list called Moderates seeks to attract ideological centrists. Extreme ideological views, both left and right, find a home. Conspiracy theorists can discuss on several conspiracy theory lists. RuMills is a list that claims to "present the truth behind the headlines" because the list's sources "are several years ahead of the rest of the world press in their predictions." Another group, Conspiracy_theorist, describes itself as a list that discusses "any and all conspiracy theories." Aryan lists advertise their network and its activities.

Some lists warn away people whom they do not want to participate on the list. One list, ActivismUSA, advises potential participants in its description that "if you're easily offended, religious, narrow-minded, or in other words, a Conservative Republican, this probably is NOT the list for you." Another list, CampusForChoice, asks that "no anti-choice individuals attempt to join this list. If we do find an anti-choicer here you will be unsubscribed immediately."[5] This exclusiveness also likely explains the appeal of mailing lists. It is easier for individuals who are like-minded to avoid others with whom they disagree.

Yet a few lists overtly see discussion as a means for improving public life. Partypolitics offers as its objective that "participants contribute to greater understanding between the several parties and views in America. We also hope to gain insight as to voter dissatisfaction with current party choices, and how people can reconnect with a sense that our political life matters." Many lists are focused on objectives such as organization and mobilization rather than discussion. For example, the list Internet-Democrats claims that its goal is to "use this powerful new tool called the Internet to build networks of Democrats in every precinct in the country and give citizens a renewed feeling of actually participating in democracy."

Bulletin Board Politics

As discussed in the first chapter, Usenet groups are categorized under domains according to the topic of the group. Most political newsgroups fall under a few hierarchies—*alt, talk, soc,* and *misc*—but increasingly they are becoming prominent in new domains as well, such as *gov* and *courts,* as well as in local, regional, and state domains.

Political newsgroups have existed since the early Internet days, even before the creation of Usenet. The early Internet, called ARPAnet (Advanced Research Projects Agency), was an arm of the Department of Defense. It included an e-mail communication system.[6] The first discussion group was fa.poli-sci, an early ARPAnet group, which eventually merged into Usenet.[7]

Early groups were oriented toward the computer science community. However, groups on other topics, including politics, emerged quickly. Groups such as talk.politics and alt.politics eventually generated other, more specialized political groups.

Political newsgroups today range from the general to the highly specific. Some of the broadly defined politically oriented groups include alt.politics.reform, alt.politics.constitution, or the even more vaguely titled alt.current-events.usa or talk.politics.misc. However, most have acquired far more specific foci. The more distinctive emphasis usually concentrates on a specific individual, organization, institution, ideology, or issue.

Like mailing lists, some political newsgroups concentrate on well-known politicians such as George W. Bush, John Kerry, or Bill Clinton (alt.politics.bush, alt.politics.kerry, and alt.politics.clinton). Other political figures are the focus at times, as evidenced by alt.rush-limbaugh and alt.fan.tom-leykis, two groups devoted to discussion of these political talk radio hosts. Some groups are directed at specific organizations such as political parties, for example, such as alt.politics.usa.republican, alt.politics.republicans, and alt.politics.democrat. Minor parties also are represented through groups such as alt.politics.greens and alt.politics.libertarian. Governmental institutions are group topics as well. Congress is the focus of alt.politics.usa.congress, while courts.usa.federal.supreme centers on the U.S. Supreme Court. The media also attract the attention of newsgroup creators. Groups such as alt.politics.media and alt.journalism devote attention to media practices and criticisms.

However, the extent of cross-posting, the absence of a moderator, and the open nature of the forums mean that even if a group is named a certain way, the discussion does not necessarily always go in that direction. Many threads, particularly those overlapping from other groups, address a wide range of topics regardless of the name of the political group.

U.S. national politics is hardly the only topic of political discussion on Usenet. Usenet is a global medium, and groups with various international emphases are common. Groups focus on regions of the world (alt.politics. europe or talk.politics.mideast) or even specific nations (alt.politics.italy, talk.politics.tibet, or alt.politics.british). Discussion can also turn to more provincial matters, such as state and local politics. One group, talk.politics. local, discusses local politics generally. But other groups, such as alabama. politics and tx.politics, talk about statewide politics, while still others, including nyc.politics and houston.politics, are devoted specifically to local-level politics.

For some groups, ideological discussion is the reason for existence. Examples include alt.society.anarchy and talk.politics.marxism. Fringe groups tend to be well represented on Usenet, with groups such as alt.politics.radical-left or alt.politics.conspiracy. However, most groups seem to revolve around specific issues, such as talk.politics.guns, talk.politics.drugs, and alt.politics. abortion. The range of issues discussed on Usenet veers from civil rights to feminism, marijuana to immigration, and on and on.

Each group is designed by the initiator to attract individuals interested in the subject as described in the title. The titles chosen by the group creator also often reveal the political bias of the list: the more specific the title, the narrower the focus of the group and perhaps the more exclusive and partisan the membership. One example was a group titled alt.impeach.clinton, which had a quite specific focus and was intended to attract users who wanted to see President Clinton impeached and removed from office. Others include alt.politics.liberal.bleed.bleed.bleed, and alt.politics.turn-left.

Specific words or letters in titles also reveal whether the group's existence is intended to support or oppose the object of discussion. Opponents of an individual or organization will organize their own Usenet groups, such as alt.politics.democrat.d, which includes discussion opposing the Democratic Party. Another guide to the group's emphasis is the use of the terms *flame* and *fan*. For example, a group titled *alt.fan.g-gordon-liddy* was created to support the talk radio host's views, whereas one with the term *flame* (such as *alt.flame.monica-lewinsky* or *alt.flame.jews*) indicates opposition.

The level of interest in groups varies greatly. Some groups, such as alt.politics.usa.republican and talk.politics.misc, attract large numbers of readers and posters. Others, however, attract little interest and limited message traffic.

Despite the plethora of groups, Usenet appears to have a distinct right-wing ideological bias.[8] Groups such as alt.usa.constitution, alt.usa.republican, alt.fan.ronald-reagan, and talk.politics.guns feature a dominant ideological strain that is decidedly rightward-leaning. Some go even further, to the extreme right, as demonstrated by groups such as alt.politics.nationalism. white and alt.politics.national-socialist.

Yet Usenet contains other points on the ideological spectrum as well. Both the center and the radical left are present. Groups such as alt. politics.democrats or alt.politics.democrats.clinton serve as a forum for a moderate leftist bent. There are also more extreme left-wing groups— alt.politics.radical left and alt.politics.socialism are examples.

The reproduction of groups is relatively easy, creating even more specialization in topical interest. General groups spawn more specific groups, such as alt.conspiracy leading to alt.conspiracy.jfk, or talk.politics to talk.politics.drugs and talk.politics.medicine.

Some groups such as soc.politics.marxism and soc.politics.anti-fascism debate radical political thought. Others center on more mainstream political views, such as alt.society.liberalism and alt.society.conservatism. Particular policy issues are the topics of a niche of political groups, such as talk.politics.drugs, talk.politics.guns, and talk.politics.medicine. The Internet itself attracts political discussion on groups such as alt.politics.data-highway and talk.politics.crypto.

Antigovernment groups appear to have a disproportionate presence on the Web. Libertarians and anarchists go to talk.politics.libertarian, alt.anarchism, or alt.society.anarchy. White supremacy groups and militias gather around groups such as alt.politics.white-power, alt.politics.nationalism.white, or misc.activism.militia.

Groups' distinctions often become muddied due to extensive cross-posting. According to one study, 21 percent of newsgroup messages are cross-posted. That number increased to one of three messages for groups devoted to American politics topics.[9] Many posters send their messages to all the groups they are subscribed to, rather than a particular one. For example, during the 2004 presidential primary season, one poster posted his message about Senator John Kerry's votes on intelligence spending on alt.politics, a generic group on politics, but also on four other groups, including alt.politics.usa and alt.politics.bush. When individuals blast a message across an array of groups, threads become more similar than distinct.

Political talk is not limited to groups with the word *politics* in the title. Others, such as soc.abortion, talk.environment, or talk.euthanasia, also feature political discussions. Even groups with nonpolitical topics also frequently have political discussions. For example, the group talk.rumors discussed rumors of the Clinton impeachment trial, Chelsea Clinton, and the private lives of presidential candidates.

Chatting About Politics

Politics is not the prime topic in Internet chat rooms. However, varieties of political chat do exist online. America Online, for example, offers chat channels such as Democrats, Republican, and Young Democrat. Since any AOL subscriber can initiate their own chat channel, the possibilities for discussion topics are endless, albeit subject to the content controls placed by America Online. Search engines such as Excite, Infoseek, and Yahoo! also sponsor their own chat rooms. For example, Yahoo! chat includes discussion in categories such as "current events" and "Washington watch."

News and political organizations also use chat for their own purposes. News organizations use chat as a way to encourage usage of their Web site. National Public Radio and the *Washington Post*, for example, have initiated chat rooms for individuals to respond to news items and to interact with politicians, journalists, political consultants, and academics. Some online groups sponsor chat from their own Web sites. For example, Town Hall, a conservative Web site at www.townhall.com, sponsors moderated chat rooms with conservative guests.

Blogging

The newest form of electronic discussion—the Web log or blog—has quickly become a forum for political opinion expression. Well-known blogs attract the attention of political activists and journalists. In fact, news organizations such as MSNBC and *Washington Monthly* have started their own blogs. The most visited political blogs include Andrew Sullivan, Daily Kos, Instapundit, and Eshaton.

Political blogs are widely read. The number one political blog—Instapundit—attracts over seventy thousand visitors a day.[10] That growth has occurred in a short time. In an eighteen-month period, Andrew Sullivan's blog went from 200,000 unique visitors a month to 379,000.[11] Political bloggers such as Andrew Sullivan, Markos Zuniga (Daily Kos), and Glenn Reynolds (Instapundit) have acquired their own exalted online discussion status. Some have even received press credentials, since their blogs have readerships that rival those of many print news outlets. For example, in 2004, for the first time, bloggers were given press credentials to the national nominating conventions.[12]

The costs of running a blog are minuscule compared to those of a traditional news organization. Bloggers have limited costs and pay expenses through a combination of advertising and donations. Blogger Andrew Sullivan, who also is an editor for the *New Republic*, reportedly raised nearly $100,000 after a pledge drive on his blog.[13]

Blogging, like other facets of political communication and online political discussion, is divided along ideological lines. While Daily Kos and TalkingPointsMemo appeal to liberals, other blogs such as Instapundit, RealClear Politics, and GOPUSA are conservative favorites. Blogging also has become a forum for candidate supporters. In 2004, Blogs for Bush, Dean Nation, and the Wesley Clark Weblog became havens for supporters of these candidates independent of each campaign's official Web site.

Blog content has impacted traditional news media and even political events. The best and earliest case was a blog repetition of a comment by Senator Trent Lott, then Senate majority leader, suggesting that the country would have been better off had Senator Strom Thurmond been elected president in 1948, when he ran as the Dixiecrat candidate on a prosegregation platform. Lott's comments were repeated by various blogs before they were finally trumpeted by traditional media. Lott apologized several times but could not make the furor go away. He subsequently resigned as Senate majority leader.[14]

But bloggers have come under criticism as self-absorbed and lacking the respect and standards of the traditional news media. According to Elizabeth Osder, "Bloggers are navel-gazers. And they're about as interesting as friends who make you look at their scrap books. There's an overfascination here with self-expression, with opinion. This is opinion without expertise, without resources, without reporting."[15]

The Process of Participation
Joining a Group or List

The availability of these forums all across the Internet and on the World Wide Web particularly means that participating in some online discussion forum has become less complicated for Internet users. Newsgroups are available through Google.

Similarly, joining a chat room usually means merely signing on to a chat channel connected to some existing Web site. Nor is anonymity breached, as it may be to a reduced extent on mailing lists or Usenet groups where an e-mail address is required. Some chat rooms, particularly those with sponsoring organizations, require real-world information, while many others, much like CB channels, request only a screen name or nickname in order to participate. Many people join a listserv from Web sites such as www.topica.com or www.lsoft.com, which specialize in providing lists of mailing lists as well as direct access to thousands of lists.

As stated earlier, joining a mailing list can be more difficult than participating in a newsgroup or a chat channel because the list may be closed and therefore intentionally exclusive. The existence of closed lists may never be known to those who do not belong to solicited groups, such as employees of a company, professionals in a network, or students in a class. Even when the list does become publicized, such as on a Web site list of lists, many list managers alert potential subscribers that they should not attempt to subscribe if they are not members of a distinct real-world community such as local union members or law enforcement officers.

Growth in the use of Internet discussion has led to the constant presence of new members of online forums. New posters are usually given instructions on how to participate and what kind of etiquette is required within the group. Some forums even require that new individuals read a contract before joining. Once they are logged on, new posters (known as "newbies") are encouraged to follow the discussion for a while before posting, in order to learn the general rules; failure to do so often evokes a harsh response from the regular participants. Newcomers sometimes ask what the group is about. One newcomer wrote, "I'd like to know what sort of news server is alt.politics economics." A reply explained that the group "deals most with news and ideas that affect the combination of politics/economics" and then explained what differentiated the group from others.

Electronic discussion is not necessarily a warm environment for new posters, however. According to Margaret L. McLaughlin, new additions to the list may not be welcomed into the community: "The frequent posters may issue a warm welcome, a rebuff, or ignore the newcomer altogether, in effect granting themselves something of an executive privilege or power with respect to entry into the community. In some groups, participation alone does not grant community membership."[16] These tendencies may be exacerbated in political groups or lists where certain individuals have come to control lists or where some individuals even create the group, list, or channel in order to promote their ideas and not those of others. Where certain ideologies predominate and the newcomer may not share them, the response may be avoidance or eventual exclusion.

Starting a Group or List

Many Internet users are taking one step beyond joining a group, list, or blog to actually creating their own online discussion forum. Practically anyone can initiate the process of creating a list or establishing a blog.

Similarly, chat channels, particularly those accessed through certain portals, can be easily constructed.

A new group, list, or channel can be on any imaginable topic. However, attracting a following of posters and lurkers is another matter. Some groups draw thousands of messages weekly, while others only sporadically receive attention or even fail to receive any notice. Many groups, mailing lists, and chat channels never attract interest and die out quickly. Others continue only as forums for their authors. One listserv—Democratic Alliance—consists almost exclusively of messages from a single individual who manages the list. The ease with which one creates a new online discussion forum obviously promotes even greater fragmentation of discussion. More and more discussion ghettoes are created where intense specialization occurs and where narrowcasting reaches its extreme.

The Nature of Political Discussion

Now that we have examined the types of political discussion online, the next question concerns the content. What exactly is being discussed online? How do people raise issues for discussion and then discuss them? How does online political discussion differ from other political discussion?

Initially, topics for discussion are set by the creators of the groups or lists, who determine what the subject of the group will be—gun control, libertarianism, Bill Clinton. The title of the group signals to potential participants the nature of the topic. But directing the discussion is a different matter. The ability of the originator to control the flow of discussion varies according to the medium. Mailing list owners can control who gets on and posts. Their power, if they wish to exercise it, can be absolute. Similarly, chat channel owners also may be able to determine discussion direction. However, newsgroup originators have little control. Beyond establishing the group and setting the broad topic in the title, they cannot block messages departing from the creator's interests.

Many forums for political discussion online—Usenet, chat, nonexclusive mailing lists—fall in the unmoderated category. In an unmoderated discussion group, no one takes an active role to stop messages or lead the discussion in accordance with the original intent of the forum creator. However, moderated groups are a growing trend, since they provide more control for the group creator over what appears online. Organizationally managed portals clearly fall in the moderated category. Online discussion forums established by Internet portals such as America Online or a news media organization are monitored and controlled by the sponsoring organization.

Participants in the newsgroup or chat channel themselves can seek to monitor discussion in other ways than denying access. Posters sometimes will urge a previous poster or posters to take their conversations to another group more pertinent to their interests. If a poster seeks to take the list in a different direction than the group or channel topic, others may protest. For example, in one political newsgroup thread, one poster noted that she and another poster were the only women participating in the thread. The second woman said she had noticed that too and asked the first if she was interested in lesbian sex. The first woman than replied that the other woman should go to a singles bar and get off the list.

Threads: The Agenda-Setting Process Imagine a telephone conversation where, after one person says something, the individual on the other end either does not respond at all or says something completely unrelated. The first person might assume the second person had not heard what was said, perhaps because he or she was distracted or the connection was bad. Even worse, perhaps the second person purposely ignored the first one.

Electronic political discussion many times looks just like that. People often ignore what others say. An individual may drop a message in the midst of a group, list, or channel with no concern over what has been said before. Newsgroups, lists, and even sometimes chat channels appear much like office bulletin boards cluttered with many messages seemingly unrelated to each other. Reading all the messages and following all the threads becomes time-consuming. Instead, participants pick and choose interesting topics as determined by the headings on messages.

The ability to say something unrelated to anything else is an obvious facet of online discussion. Unlike in a face-to-face encounter, posters of messages need not abide by the etiquette of social conversation. They can completely ignore what some other poster has said.

When actual follow-up occurs, the subsequent interaction is the discussion thread. As mentioned in the previous chapter, the initial post and the subsequent replies (and replies to replies) constitute a discussion thread. The number and length of threads have been found to vary greatly. One study found threads lasted on average from three days in one group to more than thirty-four in another, and the average number of messages in a thread was five.[17]

A thread begins when a poster initiates a discussion not already in play. This new thread usually is designated in the subject heading to differentiate it from existing topics. After a poster initiates a topic, others will respond, either immediately or over a matter of days. The thread response can be identified as such by the use of the same heading as the original messages, such as "Re: Iraq."

Threads are easy to attempt. Many individuals seek to begin a thread by posting a message with a new topic. However, few succeed. A thread requires some other participant to join the thread by responding to the original post. For example, according to Netscan, a Microsoft Usenet research site, one group (alt.politics.radical-left) in 2003 had 1,114 messages, 290 of which were initial posts, not replies. But of those, only 24 percent started threads—in other words, they were replied to by at least one other individual.[18]

Threads can be as short as two messages (the original post and a single reply) or as long as hundreds of responses and counterresponses. The length of a thread often depends on the controversy it sparks. One post titled "Why are atheists such intolerant bigots" charged that atheists manipulate history by claiming that the American founding was not based on religion. The thread continued for a month and resulted in 1,197 replies. Another message on the same group during the same period posed a question about the Fourteenth Amendment that elicited only seven responses.

Following the content of a thread can be difficult because of the practice of including in a message part or all of the text of one or more previous posts within the thread. This practice helps lurkers or future posters who may have missed the earlier post. Such content is separated visually (by italics or another device) in order to differentiate the poster's message from the message being replied to. But the poster's reply may be at the end of the previous text, which means the reader must plow through the original text in order to get to the addition. Even worse, the reply may be in pieces interspersed throughout the text of the previous post.

Posters on political groups or lists often begin a thread by including a newspaper story, a government document, an e-mail, or a post from some other group, along with their own commentary about how the news confirms their own position on some issue. Then others are expected to respond to the news story. Obviously this is less common in political chat due to the limited space available for message composition and the speed of the discussion.

Sample Threads   A glimpse at a few sample threads on political newsgroups shows how political discussion occurs via threads. One example is a thread created by a post cross-posted on two Usenet groups. Here is the initial post:

▷ Counties with ccw legislation are 84% less likely to have a multiple injury shooting than those without those provisions. And 90% less likely to have one resulting in a fatality.

Over a one-week period, this post prompted thirty-seven subsequent posts—replies and responses to replies from seventeen individuals. The first retort questioned the legitimacy of the statistics.

▷ I would be greatly interested in knowing how you obtained that information. You use statistics like a drunk uses a lamp-post, for support not illumination. I'm relatively new to the gun debate. Is CCW suppose to be an acrynom [*sic*] for Carry Concealed Weapons? Which countries are you talking about? What study are you citing?

The next post (not from the original post author but from another participant) satirizes the first respondent:

▷ I'm relatively new to the gun debate.
But you already know that Fred here is posting bogus stats, or that he doesn't understand them? What a remarkable display of intellectual prowess.

▷ Is CCW suppose to be an acrynom [sic] for Carry Concealed Weapons?
Concealed Carry of Weapon laws.

▷ Which countries are you talking about?
Check again. He said counties. In this case, comparing results in all 3000+ U.S. counties over a period of 15+ years.

▷ What study are you citing?
John Lott and David Mustard's University of Chicago study on concealed carry laws and violent crime: Crime, Deterrence, and Right-to-Carry Concealed Handguns by John R. Lott and David B. Mustard. (You should be able to download a PDF or other file format version from: http://papers.ssrn.com/paper.taf?abstract_id=161637) Lott's recent book, "More Guns, Less Crime" covers the material fairly thoroughly.

Given the time lag between writing and posting and posting and responses, individual posters often post again without having seen any responses from others. In this case, the first respondent, who challenged the original post, then continues with another post questioning the content of the message heading of the original post:

▷ I have a second question that I just thought of, why did you entitle this post "Gun Control Kills School Children"? Do you want kids to arm themselves. I think that would work great, don't you? Little Billy can be off to school and his mom will ask right before he gets on the bus "Billy, did you eat breakfast?"
▷ "Yeah Mom"
▷ "Do you have your books?"
▷ "Yeah Mom"
▷ "Okay-don't forget your nine"
▷ Gun people are scary

At this point, still another poster joins the fray by responding to that post, particularly the last statement:

▷ No, it's just that antigun people are abysmally stupid, as your little
▷ "Billy" scenario has amply illustrated.

Another poster also responded to the same post by claiming that the previous poster has demonstrated "your inability to think analytically . . . In this case, anyone with even half a brain (you're somewhere under 1/8, by my full-brained estimation) can figure out that what is meant is that ADULTS who supervise kids could be armed."

As interest in the thread increased, responses then began to fragment into different directions. Some posters focused on Israel's policies. One suggested readers go to a Web site discussing the Israeli experience. But another responded that "Israel is one of those countries which uses torture on an 'administrative basis.' It seems that as though their answer to everything is violence." Then several messages veered into a discussion of whether Israel is racist. Others addressed whether teachers should be armed, with the first respondent reentering that argument. One exchange included sparring about who was worse—gun advocates or gun-control supporters. Still others argued about whether criminals prefer guns to other weapons.

The thread lasted longer than most, but similarly died out as the discussion participants seemed to tire of the discussion and leave. An unusual fact about this thread was the originator's failure to join in the subsequent discussion. A more common phenomenon is the poster defending his (or perhaps occasionally her) initial post against criticism from others.

Several behaviors were evident in this thread. Posters commonly sought to use evidence to support truth claims. However, the reliance on this evidence ranged from highly specific sources ("according to the Bureau of Justice Statistics publication NCJ-148201") to vague references ("a study done some years back by a student at Sonoma State," "FBI stats," or "I can only go by accounts by a personal friend").

Calls for more evidence also appeared. When one poster argued that Switzerland is not the paragon of safety and gun ownership often claimed, another asked, "You got ANY evidence that Switzerland isn't 'a quintessential example of safety and guns coexisting.'"

Some posters moved from the specific to the general, making generalizations followed up by broad accusations. Gun advocates, gun-control enthusiasts, Israel, teachers' unions, and other groups were given stereotypical treatment. Gun advocates became "scary." Gun-control enthusiasts were "abysmally stupid." Israelis were "racists." The media invariably were "liberal."

Personal attacks on other posters became common. When one poster compared arming teachers with *Rambo*, a reply commented: "You think that movies actually reflect real life." Another charged that a previous poster should "learn some about the subject, or just admit you aren't interested in anything but your own opinion."

An example of a briefer thread is the following post that was cross-posted on four groups:

▷ If K-Mart can sell guns over the counter, why can't I legally buy a little marijuana? Who's to blame for this hypocritical inconsistency regarding responsible adults? Why should violence be a lower priority than narcotics? I want answers. For a related laugh, check out . . . http://www.womenweaponsandweed.com . . . the site that'll make Tipper fume.

In three days, the thread grew to eleven responses posted on the group. Subsequent posts essentially agreed with the initial post. One wrote, "K-mart should sell anything anyone wants to buy, be it marijuana or guns. Laws that directly effect [sic] business are bad, socialist, and counter productive." Another responded, "Adults should be able to buy whatever they wish to. . . . If I wanna buy guns, dope, cyanide, etc., that's my business and K-Mart should be able to sell those things to me if they choose to."

One response answered sarcastically: "Yeah, I don't see why I can't buy a nuclear bomb or some anthrax at my local Kmart." Then a poster sarcastically responded to that message by writing, "I'm actually all for the availability of the 'Home Nuke,' if Mutually Assured Destruction can work for States, why not for the individual?"

A reply from another poster snidely commented, "Great, another role-player." The poster who made the remark about the "Home Nuke" then replied, "Gosh . . . I hardly know what to say. Is this directed at my attempt at levity, or are you simply being dismissive toward me in particular? And if one were to occasionally engage in a bit of roleplaying, where's the harm in that?"

The thread ended with a post from "Billy," who answered the question "If K-Mart can sell guns over the counter, why can't I legally buy a little marijuana" with the reply "Because it gives Rosie O'Donnell the munchies, and she's trying to keep her girlish figure."

As these examples show, threads can degenerate quickly and head down unrelated paths. They can die out due to lack of interest on the part of the posters. Facetiousness is difficult to communicate online. Whether the initial poster was serious is hard to tell. However, some of the posters treated the post as a serious commentary, while others assumed it was a joke.

There is no requirement to keep a certain discussion on track. Another example of a subject gone awry is the following post, which was cross-posted on several lists:

▷ You will win. An honest politician is exceedingly hard to find.
   And we've had enough of the Republocrats. You're the man.

The post is for Jesse and is urging him to run. The identity of "Jesse" is not explicitly stated; however, the poster probably is referring to former Minnesota governor Jesse Ventura and the office is likely that of president. The third sentence's reference to "Republocrats" suggests Ventura rather than another politician involved in one of the two major parties, such as Jesse Jackson.

One might expect subsequent posts on this thread to address some of the points raised in the original post: Could Ventura win? Is he "an honest politician"? Are the Republicans and the Democrats essentially the same, as the poster implies? Yet the thread quickly moved far from the points raised in the original post. The first response, perhaps assuming that "Jesse" referred to Jesse Jackson, attacked Martin Luther King Jr. as an insurrectionist who abandoned his civil disobedience policy. The next three responses argued whether insurrection was necessarily violent. The main theme of the original post was quickly lost, and even the main point of the first reply was discarded by the next posters.

Threads can go anywhere. Replies need not address the main point of the original message nor even secondary points raised by the original poster. Often, respondents concentrate on a factual error stated by a previous poster, thereby ignoring any argument made. In fact, many times subsequent posters will treat an existing thread as an opportunity to begin an original thread, perhaps since there is already interest in the topic.

The close of a thread does not mean that the discussion is over. A poster later may raise the same issue, but with a new thread. Or several simultaneous threads basically on the same subject can be extant at once.

Cross-postings News dissemination on Internet political discussion is like a prairie wildfire. The technique that accelerates news transmission is crossposting. News spreads quickly due to the tendency to cross-post. Crossposting, as mentioned earlier, is the practice of posting a message simultaneously on more than one newsgroup or mailing list. When the number of groups or lists cross-posted to is voluminous, then the practice is called spamming.

For posters who want wide distribution of their messages, cross-posting does the trick. A poster can quickly spread details of a current news story supporting his or her position or release information about an upcoming event he or she wants others on various newsgroups to be aware of. However, cross-posting also has its disadvantages. Rumors and misinformation spread as rapidly as truth. It is difficult to correct widely spread misinformation.

Another effect is on the quality of discourse online. Because both original posters and those responding will cross-post on the same lists, the same threads will occur on several groups concurrently. That contributes to the disjointed nature of discussion. Topics more germane to one list nevertheless will be thrust into another. Individuals who spam messages will be seeking not discussion but distribution for their views. Such behavior is more appropriate for an announce list, yet it is common on Usenet. Cross-posting is less common on moderated mailing lists because the list manager can screen out messages designed as spam. It is also uncommon on chat, where one must post the same message repeatedly on each chat channel, a more time-consuming practice than merely adding newsgroups or e-mail addresses in the message header.

Nondiscussion Posts

Discussion is not the only content on these online forums. Electronic political talk also has become the venue for posts that are designed not for discussion but for information and potential action by readers. As mentioned in Chapter 1, two types of mailing lists are announce and discussion lists. Announce lists are popular among political organizations because they offer an opportunity to communicate with group members or other interested parties. It is similar to sending a mailing or a periodical to the members, but on a more frequent basis, such as weekly or even daily.

Online groups use discussion lists to broadcast regular information about the group and its activities. Established interest groups use sympathetic newsgroups to pass around information designed for readers who do not belong to the interest group but who may share the interest group's objectives.

One example is the Rainforest Action Network, as shown by the following post:

▷ Greetings Activists!
Wanted to send you all out a copy of the March 17th Call to Action to Demonstrate Against Home Depot. Some of you may have seen it but please pass it on to other networks, friends, allies etc. The word is just in. Home Depot has unveiled their long awaited environmental policy and it's a complete scam! It doesn't even address the issue of old growth forests. This means they need to hear from each and every one of us. We need demonstrations at their stores everywhere so that they know that grassroots activists are not going to tolerate them profiting from the liquidation of the world's last remaining old growth forests! Organize a demonstration for the 17th today! Let us know as soon as you know if/ where you are doing an event, who the local contact is (for both the media and activists that contact us to be in involved in your event) phone, email and snail mail. For more information you can reach me at the 1-800-989-RAIN number below or at rags@ran.org. Keep up all the great work and keep in touch.
In solidarity, - Patrick, RAN

The message also urged recipients to forward the post to other groups in order to increase its circulation.

But announce lists are not the only places where these types of messages appear. Groups also are using discussion lists as well as Usenet groups in order to announce instead of discuss. Even individuals sometimes use online discussion not to initiate discussion threads but to broadcast their views to an audience.

One individual, who calls himself or herself "The Survivalist," regularly posts a WorldNet daily news alert. The intent is not to commence a thread but to broadcast news the individual views as important for others to know. Often such people are using online forums to draw attention to their Web pages or blogs, where they post lengthier online exposition of their views. Such advertising gives their ideas a broader exposure. The following cross-posted Usenet message is an example of such a tactic:

▷ The street plan of Washington D.C. was drawn up by the well known French Architect, Revolutionary, Occultist, & Freemason Lafeyette.
There is a Pentagram incorporated into the main arteries surrounding the White House.
The 5 pointed pentagram is often imposed over a drawing of a goats's head, an important occult symbol.
The monumental white temple building of the Supreme Council 33rd Degree, Mother Council of the World lies precisely 13 blocks north of the White House at 1733 Sixteenth Ave. N.W.
It's placement over the pentagram forms the "crown" of the "goat's head."
Freemasonry routinely misuses public funds in secret to propagate it's society by incorporating it's various gang symbols into public building's, monuments, seals, and currency.
Is the public aware when a new monument is dedicated that a hidden compartment often lies at it's base containing masonic accoutraments?
No.
If they were aware of this practice of "dedicating" via a masonic occult baptism of their public edifices and monuments would they approve?
No.
That is why Freemasonry keeps this practice secret
Even though many non-masons in positions in public trust are aware of this practice they fear the loss of their jobs or their person if they would come foreward. [Sic]
Please visit my new web site Masonic Education—Our Founding Fathers at the bottom of this post. Click on the 3rd chapter for the specific case of Lafeyette and the Pentagram of Washington D.C.
Fraternally Yours,
St. John the Sublime Reformer
A Certain Point Within A Circle
Masonic Historian

Common Discussion Topics

Beyond announcements, what do these participants in online forums spend so much time actually talking about? Discussion can be divided into four broad categories: current events, folklore, philosophical debate, and political action.

Current Events Many newsgroups, mailing lists, and chat rooms concentrate their discussion on the events of the day, such as the example at the beginning of this chapter of posts commenting on the announcement of the death of Senator Paul Wellstone of Minnesota. But other events could be U.S. military involvement abroad, the latest government scandal, congressional action, presidential decisions, Supreme Court opinions, and so on.

Current events become discussion fodder because they are new. Discussion on existing topics can wane due to lack of interest. Threads wear out after a while because the same arguments have been made over and over again. Current events offer a new opportunity to pursue an old theme. Gun control advocates can argue for gun control measures in the wake of school shootings. Opponents of the current administration can use a recent action as new ammunition for more criticism. Current events become particularly susceptible to new threads if they mesh with the existing emphasis of the group. Examples would be a government scandal for a conspiracy theory list or a wave of school shootings for a gun discussion newsgroup.

For people who work at home, which is a growing phenomenon, the online discussion of current events may be the equivalent of gathering around the office water cooler or lounging in the break room. It offers them an opportunity to bounce what they have learned off others while getting interpersonal reaction as well.

The emphasis on current events also demonstrates the importance of traditional media to many political posters. Posters of new threads often point to news stories as the impetus for their posts. Many times the poster will actually enclose some or all of the text of a news story to stimulate discussion. Posters often cite from the *New York Times*, the *Los Angeles Times*, the *Wall Street Journal*, and other elite news sources. Given the conservative slant of many newsgroups, other possible sources are conservative-oriented news media sources such as the *Washington Times* or the *American Spectator*.

One sample below—the entire body of a Usenet message—shows this custom:

From Roll Call, 7/22/99:
http://www.rollcall.com/newsscoops/leadscoop.html
Rachel Van Dongen
Party-switching Rep. Mike Forbes (N.Y.) was embraced by House
Democrats yesterday, when he attended his first meeting of the
Democratic Caucus, and was greeted with multiple standing ova-
tions and promises of help in his 2000 re-election battle. Closer to
the end of neanderthal rule in the House.
Harry

This practice also suggests that posters may well be individuals who are
highly attuned to traditional news media sources. Rather than using new
Internet information sources, particularly online forums, as a substitute
for traditional news media, they appear to be heavy consumers of traditional news offerings.

But new online information sources also are touted. As mentioned
above, some posters use their posts to attract readers to various Web sites.
These may be sites established by individuals or little known groups seeking to provide an alternative view of news. For example:

▷   You want action. I want action. Enter Stage Right has action! And
     now every week!
     This week's edition of Enter Stage Right is out now and with two
     new writers! Check it at http://www.enterstageright.com

Folklore   The emphasis of some posts is on events that the posters think
have been deliberately suppressed by the traditional news media. These
events, however, often fall in the category of online folklore, that is, rumors
circulating among online discussants that may or may not be reliable information. For example, people discuss sightings of flying saucers or rumors
that government agencies tap their cellular phones. Some groups such as
alt.folklore.urban or alt.folklore.ghost-stories are specifically devoted to such
discussions.

But folklore also circulates widely in political groups. ABC News
reporter Pierre Salinger reported that he had received a classified document that "proved" TWA flight 800's fiery crash was caused by a U.S. Navy
missile. However, the revelation was not new to many Internet users
because Salinger's "original" secret document actually was an e-mail message written on America Online by a former airline pilot and distributed
on the Internet for several months before Salinger's pronouncement.[19]

Damaging but often untrue information about well-known individuals
is circulated via the Internet. For example, in the wake of the release of the

Starr Report in 1998 with its lurid details of a sexual relationship between President Clinton and Monica Lewinsky, a message circulated around the Internet claiming that Kenneth Starr had said in a 1987 interview on *60 Minutes:* "Public media should not contain explicit or implied descriptions of sex acts. Our society should be purged of the perverts who provide the media with pornographic material while pretending it has some redeeming social value under the public's right to know." The quote was an Internet hoax. However, since it sounded like something Starr might have said, and it was embarrassing in light of the content of the Starr Report, it was widely circulated through online political forums.

But sometimes folklore circulated in online discussion forums acquires traction in the traditional media real-world validity. For example, the story of an Arkansas woman who claimed Bill Clinton had raped her while he was Arkansas attorney general circulated widely through Usenet political groups before it appeared in traditional news media stories. However, only when the story appeared in the *Wall Street Journal* did it receive widespread traditional news media distribution.

Philosophical Discussion   Some political groups are more interested in long-running ideological disputes than in the current events of the day. Participants spend countless hours posting messages discussing the virtues of socialism over capitalism, or libertarian philosophy. Groups such as alt.politics.radical-left, soc.politics.marxism, and talk.politics.libertarian are devoted to discussion of ideology. They debate the role of Stalin in Marxism-Leninism, the distinctions between communism and fascism, or the application of libertarian dogma in political life.

Obviously there is some overlap between political philosophy and current events, since current events often become the stimulus to return to the broader philosophical issues since they can be utilized as argument supports in the ongoing discussion. But current events become tangential, or at best supportive, of the ongoing sweeping philosophical debate.

Political Action   As mentioned earlier, some lists and groups are designed to foment political action rather than analyze ideologies or merely comment on current events. These groups use their discussion space to debate how best to carry out their shared political goals. These may include discussion about whether the pro-life movement should pursue a wholesale agenda or focus on particular issues such as partial-birth abortion laws. As another example, immediately following Republican presidential candidate Pat Buchanan's announcement that he was joining the Reform Party, one conservative mailing list owner used his list to announce that he would be supporting Buchanan as a Reform Party candidate and urged all his list subscribers to do the same.

A Study of Four Groups

One way of analyzing political content of electronic discussion forums is by examining a sample of message content of specific forums. In order to obtain a sample of discussion postings, all messages in four political Usenet groups were selected for study. These groups were alt.politics.radical-left, alt.politics.clinton, alt.politics.usa.constitution, and alt.politics.usa.republican. The total message content of these four groups during two periods (June 14–20, 1997, and October 25–30, 1999) was examined. The first three groups were analyzed during the first period. The fourth group was added and studied alone during the second period. The objective was to conduct an ethnographic description of a small sample of groups. (See the Appendix for more on methodology.)

These particular groups were selected for several reasons: (1) They are clearly political groups. Each contains the word *politics* in the title. Moreover, their actual content is explicitly and almost exclusively political. (2) They are among the most active among political groups, with a large number of daily posts. (3) They represent a cross-section of Usenet political discussion. The first two Usenet groups represent the ideological left and the second two the right. Moreover, there is variety within each category, as the first of the two groups in each category generally represents a more extreme ideological viewpoint. Hence there are two more extreme groups (alt.politics.radical-left and alt.politics.usa.constitution) and two more centrist groups (alt.politics.clinton and alt.politics.usa.republican).

They were active in the sense that there was a significant amount of message traffic between individuals during this period of study. Message traffic for each group was as follows: 711 messages on alt.politics.radical-left, 743 for alt.politics.clinton, 232 on alt.politics.constitution, and 1,416 messages on alt.politics.usa.republican.

Setting the Agenda

As in offline conversations, posters vary significantly in the extent of their participation in the conversation. A few people dominate the discussion. A study of participation in one Usenet group found that two-thirds of the posters posted less than ten times, while one poster contributed one-quarter of all the messages.[20] Another analysis of a listserv group similarly found that three-fifths of the 703 posters posted only one to three messages each, while three posters wrote one-fifth of all messages.[21]

TABLE 2.1 Select Characteristics of Political Newsgroup Messages

	Responses to Other Posts (%)	Flaming (%)	Attack on Third Party (%)	Evidence References (%)
Constitution	68	37	28	9
Radical-Left	90	62	37	13
Republican	94	33	20	10
Clinton	87	11	8	12

The dominance of a few is enhanced by the failure on the part of active posters to reach out to others. Occasionally posters will encourage a previous poster to reply again, particularly if they feel the previous poster is being silent because he or she has been bested in argument and does not wish to admit it. But on the whole, there is little attempt to include lurkers.

Not surprisingly, in these four groups a few people led the discussion. Most posted messages were responses to previous messages, as Table 2.1 demonstrates. Most responded to existing threads rather than attempt to initiate new threads.

Thread origination was most common within the alt.politics.usa.constitution group. The posters on that group were more likely to seek to set the agenda than to follow one already set. But even in the Constitution group, more than two-thirds of the messages followed up on existing threads.

Most participants, then, follow along with existing discussions. Though anyone could attempt to start a thread, others, probably the small number of regulars in the group, would determine whether a thread was actually picked up and continued. Many attempted discussions never materialize because the initial message received little or no response from others.[22]

The Agenda

What were the topics of discussion on this sample of four groups? In order to use a standard categorization of issues, the "most important issues" classification created by the Harris Survey was employed to the categorization of topics of discussion threads. (See Appendix.) The results are shown in Table 2.2.

The agendas for the discussion threads rarely discussed these policy issues. The most commonly discussed policy issue was gun control. Race relations, crime/ violence, and the economy received minimal attention. There was almost no discussion of education, taxes, health care, U.S. foreign policy, the environment, and a host of other policy issues.

TABLE 2.2 Issue Agendas of Threads

	% of threads addressing specific topic			
	Clinton	Constitution	Radical Left	Republican
Education	0	0	0	1
Crime/violence	0	0	21	2
Taxes	2	0	0	1
Health care	1	0	0	1
Social security	2	0	0	0
Gun control	11	20	14	11
Economy	1	10	0	2
Budget deficit	0	0	0	1
Foreign policy	1	0	7	6
Drugs	0	0	0	1
Welfare	0	0	0	1
Defense	0	0	0	1
Ethics in government	4	0	0	4
Abortion	3	0	0	2
Medicare	0	0	0	1
Homelessness	1	0	0	1
Environment	0	0	0	3
Impeachment	11	0	0	1
Religion	0	20	0	3
Peace/nuclear arms	5	0	0	3
Civil rights	0	0	0	1
Immigration	0	0	0	4
Race relations	4	0	7	1
Terrorism	3	0	0	1
Other	50	50	50	46
Total	99*	100	99*	99*
N =	111	10	14	178

* Rounding error

The largest category was "other" because a large proportion of the discussion threads (about 50 percent) addressed generally nonpolicy issues. "Other" included a wide array of topics such as the 2000 presidential election, the upcoming expected New York Senate race between New York May or Rudolph Giuliani and First Lady Hillary Clinton, the recent death of Republican Senator John Chafee of Rhode Island, proposed limits on executive orders, and a controversial art exhibit in New York City. A common "other" topic was general disparaging remarks about either liberals or conservatives (depending on the posters).

The fact that there were up to 178 threads on a newsgroup in the course of one week, most of them running simultaneously, suggests one major obstacle to discussion. Due to the existence of several threads running simultaneously, the discussion is not always easy to follow. One study found the average number of simultaneous threads on a group was three to four daily.[23]

Spam

Discussion also is hampered by the great amount of clutter on Usenet groups, caused primarily by the practice of spamming. Spam, unsolicited promotional messages, is a growing problem on Usenet groups. The vast majority of spams are commercial, but some are political.[24] Increasingly, individuals are spamming political groups with porn site solicitations.

Discussion threads become more difficult to sustain when they are interspersed with so many other messages posted with no intent to start a conversation. These included spams from various organizations such as the Institute for Public Accuracy or even the White House, which sends daily posts to select newsgroups. News organizations, such as ABC News and CNN, are sending news stories or press releases via posts to various groups. Even some candidates are advertising themselves via spam on Usenet.

Cross-posting was the norm on these discussion groups. Only 6 out of 3,102 posts were not cross-posted (see Table 2.3). Two-thirds of the messages were posted to between six and twenty other groups. Cross-posting

TABLE 2.3 Message Cross-Posting by Group

Number of Messages Cross-posted to:	Clinton (%)	Constitution (%)	Radical-Left (%)	Republican (%)	Total (%)
No groups	0	1	0	0	0
1–5 groups	27	27	33	27	28
6–10 groups	25	39	14	44	32
11–20 groups	39	33	49	25	35
21+ groups	10	0	4	3	5
Totals	101*	100	100	99	100
N =	743	232	711	1,416	3,102

* Rounding error

to many other groups was most common on alt.politics.radical-left. Over
half of the posts on that group were posted to at least eleven other groups.

Cross-posting was not unique to the period studied. According to
Netscan, the Microsoft Usenet research site, 93 percent of the messages
on alt.politics.usa.constitution in 2003 were also posted on alt.poli-
tics.usa.republican.[25]

Flames

Daniel Burston and David Kline write, "Out on the digital frontier, you
can pretty much do whatever you want—and, for the most part, there's no
sheriff or posse to stop you."[26] That was true of these Usenet groups. Posters could say whatever they wished, for good or ill.

A common complaint of Usenet messages is their vitriolic nature, particularly those posted to political groups. One study of standards of behavior on Usenet postings of five newsgroups over a three-week period found
that 272 individuals were disciplined for various infractions of Usenet
conduct.[27] Flaming has become a pejorative term for verbal attacks on
other posters' ideas as well as on them personally. The problem of flaming
has become so acute that legal scholars are now addressing the amount of
liability group moderators have when posters defame each other.[28]

On these four groups, flaming was a common practice. The degree of
negativism varied across these four groups. The group alt.politics.radical-
left was the most negative (see Table 2.1). The least vicious was alt.poli-
tics.clinton, where the lack of attacks may have been due to the group's
apparent role as a gathering place for Clinton supporters. Perhaps the type
of people who are attracted to particular groups moderated the tone of the
discussion.

One form of attack targeted the ideas espoused by other posters. For
example, one writer termed his opponent's views "pseudo-intellectual flot-
sam." Another opined that "conservatives have been cloning themselves
for years. Ever notice how they repeat the same dumb arguments over and
over?" Still another concluded that he did not have "time for such Mickey
Mouse drivel." Some of the criticism centered on the presentation of the
argument: "You're long on bluster and short on argument. Provide something less generalized than 'thriving,' 'most new jobs,' 'a great deal of.'"

The attacks in posted messages could be directed at third parties, such
as institutions (Congress, the United Nations), then-current elected officials (Bill Clinton, Newt Gingrich, or Al Gore), organized groups (ACLU,
gun lobby), or broad groupings (conservatives, liberals, gays). For example, one writer took on both an institution and an unorganized group:
"The EC [European Economic Community] is another economic power

block looking for its piece of action at the expense of weaker power blocks. 'One worlders' need to get their heads out of the clouds and look at the world as it really is." Another message from a different poster maligned another group: "No one needs to revel in ignorance. Except, of course, Republicans." Overall, slightly more than one of five (21.8 percent) of the posts included such comments. They were most common in alt.politics. radical-left, where 37 percent of the messages did so.

But much of the flaming is reserved for the other message posters. Again, of the four groups studied, alt.politics.radical-left was the most vitriolic. More than three-fifths of posts in that group included attacks on previous posters. More than one-third of the alt.politics.constitution group posts were similarly attack-oriented. Only the alt.politics.clinton group avoided much criticism of others who participated in the group (see Table 2.1).

The extent of flaming on alt.politics.radical-left may be attributable to the intensity of the conflict there. The seeming conservative dominance of Usenet groups means that many political Usenet posters from the right gravitate to this group in order to engage in ideological warfare with those on the left. Where better to find people with whom to argue? Some posters acted as if they wanted to dominate whatever group was out there on Usenet, regardless of the initial focus of the group.

A common feature of flaming was the ad hominem attack. Often these attacks questioned the intelligence of the poster: "Your comment simply illustrates ignorance." "Keep your stereotypes to yourself! They will keep your little mind company." "Of course that's too deep for a shallow person like yourself." "You shouldn't just rely on books you read in grade school." "How can anyone have an intelligent debate with an illiterate?" "Let me guess . . . you're a product of public schooling, aren't you?" "You are, as usual, confused."

Some posters sought to embarrass others in front of the group. One poster wrote that another poster "has urged people to call the same senators multiple times. In other words, he is telling people to make fraudulent phone calls on behalf of the Republicans." The same poster was charged with spamming "the same Usenet article with accusations against Clinton from a Right-wing smear book 250 times over a period of a week or so."

Name-calling was a frequent tactic in these Usenet political discussion posts. For example, other ideas or groups of individuals were often reduced to simple monikers such as "gunloons" or "oneworlders": "This is the kind of argument expected from the pro-coat hanger crowd." "The GOP is the party of bigoted morons." "It never occurs to gunloons that guns had lots to do with making those tragedies possible. Could the Nazis or Bolsheviks have done their work without lots of guns? How about John

Hinckley or Lee Harvey Oswald or Colin Fletcher?" "You jackbootlicking apologist for government mass murder." "Typical leftist mindset." "Oh, grow up and try not to be so sexist." "You're not another one of those Chinese funded B2B agitprop whores, are you?"

Some of these attacks targeted well-known individuals: "More people have been killed by Ted Kennedy's Oldsmobile than by any of my firearms." "Stupid people shouldn't breed . . . they end up giving birth to things like Ralph Nader."

Bill Clinton has probably been the most reviled well-known individual on Usenet. These groups were no exception. Various message posters called him "philanderer-in-chief," "slick Willie," and "low life dirtbag." One poster claimed Clinton "doesn't have an ethical/moral bone in his body not to mention his pathological lying."

But verbal denunciations also are frequently directed at other participants in the group: "You are a fine example of what I detest." Flaming also included an effort to close off debate. Occasionally, some group members explicitly tried to shut down discussion by running others off the discussion list or discouraging them from posting. The following examples are illustrative of this point: "Should we even bother to read these any more, Roger? I mean, the last ones you posted were lies, or inaccurate, so can you give us some assurance that you are at least checking them out before you post them?" "[G]o quietly, and do not speak about that which you do not know." "Are you so arrogant that you believe everything you say should be read by everyone whether they are interested or not?"

Regulars sometimes put down less-frequent posters. One regular admonished another poster: "[I]if you hadn't merely butted into the middle of this thread, you would have realized that this thread is bigger than you think." Another reminded a previous poster that "the post you're responding to is over a month old, and you've taken it completely out of context." Still another complained that "people in general who post to the net ought to learn how to read a header."

One might conclude that flaming would be made easier by use of an alias. When people subscribe to a newsgroup they can choose whether or not to use their real names or some other designation. Many decided not to include a name. In this study, eleven percent of the messages carried no name. However, some posters preferred an alias rather than using their real names. Names such as Dingicat or Black Adder serve as aliases. Others such as Xona are unclear. Their e-mail address still appeared, and it is possible to tell something about the poster by their e-mail address. Yet e-mail addresses also can be manufactured to cloak identity. It is hard for other participants to identify specific individuals from addresses such as obi-wan@richsoft.demon, superspy@worldnet.att.net, or somebody@any-where.com.

On the four Usenet groups studied, there were 2,759 messages where a name was present. Of those, 18 percent had clear aliases. Another 11 percent were unclear. These included e-ail addresses such as papabudge@aol.com. Many posters did not mind others—posters or lurkers—knowing exactly who they were, as they included a signature including their full names, addresses, occupations, and other information. They become "one of the most immediate and visually forceful cues to identity."[29]

Use of aliases varied across these groups. Of the four Usenet groups studied, use of online aliases was most common in alt.politics.usa.constitution, where 22 percent of the participants operated using an alias. Of course, even the presence of an actual discernible name does not necessarily mean it is not an alias. Any name can be created. For example, males could post as females and vice versa.

Assuming that most names are legitimate, this result would suggest that 64 percent of those posting are using clearly identifiable names. That means a majority of those participating are willing to use what is likely their own name. However, a significant minority may be reluctant to do so.

Anonymity on the part of some users can become frustrating for other users. Other posters occasionally sought more information about such people. For example, one poster asked another jokingly, "Are you really Dennis Rodman in drag?"

People acquire new personalities in online discussions. Chat rooms are filled with odd names adopted by people to mask their real names and identities. Such aliases can prevent people from being spammed. Also, it may reduce unwanted offline contact. However, it also offers the opportunity to appear to be someone different online. People come to be identified not for who they really are, but by their frequent postings in their online identities.

Yet the hypothesis that people who use aliases are more likely to flame is not true. Those who used an alias were not more likely to flame than those who did not. People who flamed did not tend to hide behind aliases in order to do so. Flamers actually may want to make their identities readily known to others within the group so that they can be recognized and acquire a reputation. According to Judith S. Donath, "Reputation is enhanced by contributing remarks of the type admired by the group."[30] For some groups, those remarks may be flames.

Flaming also may be an attribute of the male-dominated nature of these Usenet groups. For 1,861 messages, a name was present and gender could be determined. Of those, only 6 percent were female. It is possible that females were more likely than males to use aliases, but there is no evidence to suggest that would happen. The alt.politics.constitution group had the smallest number of messages from women—only two, or just over 1 percent. That group also had the highest proportion of people with clear aliases.

Still another explanation is the nature of computer-mediated communication. The lack of a face and the accompanying nonverbal cues makes flaming easier. The absence of certain emotional caveats—a wink, a nod, or some other qualifying signals—may overemphasize the seriousness of the written comments.

Evidence

The ease of cutting and pasting, as well as attachments and hot links, heightens the capability to bolster rhetorical arguments with the texts of supporting documentation. The electronic network becomes a convenient means for individuals to download and attach various documents.[31] Posters sometimes did paste into their messages the texts of news stories from various media sources such as the *New York Times*, the *Washington Post*, and other major newspapers.

Yet, surprisingly, many posters omitted supporting evidence. Posters usually based their arguments on their own authority. The political discussion usually lacked external evidence that would stimulate further investigation of the topic and allow other posters to test the claimant's assertions. Few posters actually made reference to specific supporting materials such as books, articles, or reports (see Table 2.1). Some posters made vague references to reports and statistics. One wrote, for example, that "there are stats that tell how much each passenger on an airplane is worth." However, since more specific information was not provided, readers could not independently verify the poster's claims.

Some provide a source, but with no citation. For example one poster claimed the *St. Petersburg Times* said that a prominent CNN law commentator had contributed money to the campaigns of Democratic Party candidates. However, no specific date was provided.

This lack of supporting evidence became a frequent source of criticism by other posters. One poster responded to a post: "How do you know [many people have an innate instinct to oppose homosexuality or interracial marriage]?" Another asked a previous poster to "provide your backup for stating that the word 'people' in the Constitution means the 'State.'" "If you're going to post such allegations, please have the courtesy to provide at least a speck of verifiable evidence."

For some posters, the reference to supporting evidence was to their own Web site. For example, one poster wrote that "Clinton is a Mason. For proof of a real life conspiracy and Freemasonry, visit my Web site at . . ." Again, the Usenet group post becomes another advertising venue for drawing attention to one's own Web page in order to show that evidentiary information actually is available.

Online Discussion as Political Forum

Although the political world of electronic discussion is varied, ostensibly appealing to every taste, and becoming involved is not difficult, online political talk is neither necessarily democratic nor even participatory.[32] It fails to include. In fact, it can expressly exclude. It features dominance by a few, who consciously act to maintain that hegemony.

One commentator on electronic discussion concluded that "much of what passes for political discussion can best be compared to two teenage siblings in the heat of argument: 'Did not! Did so! Did not! Did so!' And so forth."[33] Public electronic political discussion comes with great promise for facilitating public dialogue and expanding political participation. Yet the reality is much less sanguine.

Electronic discussion, in its current form, is a far cry from the ideal political forum. As Theodore Roszak has noted: "The electronic bulletin boards, in which some see adumbrations of a new democratic forum, are also frequently taken up with trivial or less-than-idealistic pursuits: dating services, jokes, ticket sales, soap opera summaries, investing, and, more and more often, shopping."[34]

But even when electronic discussion focuses on politics, the picture is not much better. Online discussion more closely resembles the *Jerry Springer Show* rather than National Public Radio or CNN. In political discussions, people often talk past one another when they are not verbally attacking each other. Posters quickly launch into rhetorical excess followed by broadsides against the groups or individuals they have long despised. Too often, when others disagree with them, they begin to attack them personally—questioning their intelligence, lumping them with others they dislike, and, ultimately, snidely dismissing them.

Such a forum is more than mere opinion sharing, although electronic discussion stumbles even in that role.[35] The emphasis is not on problem solving but on discussion dominance. Such behavior does not resemble deliberation and it does not encourage participation, particularly by the less politically interested.

CHAPTER **3**

Online Discussants

A famous *New Yorker* cartoon shows two dogs, one sitting on a chair in front of a computer. The first dog says to the other, explaining why he is sitting at the computer, "On the Internet, no one knows you are a dog."

Though computer-mounted cameras may become a standard feature in future online discussion, currently users can be identified only by the written word. Electronic political discussion allows a high degree of anonymity. In fact, that is a highly appealing feature of Internet discussion for many users. The lengths to which some people go to be anonymous on the Internet suggests that the online discussant is an anonymous, seemingly unknowable individual who sits at a computer screen typing messages read by thousands but who is personally known to few.

In reality, those who discuss online are not as anonymous as they think. We actually know quite a bit about people who talk to others in discussion forums. We may not be able to identify individuals, but based on survey research, we can draw portrayals of Internet discussion participants and also compare them with other online users.[1]

In this chapter, we will sketch such portraits of the online conversation community. First, we examine the two groups—online discussants and others online—in terms of demographics such as age, gender, income, and other factors. Then we will explore their computer and online usage and determine how different they are as computer users from others online. Next we will look at them as media consumers and address specifically the question of whether online discussion has supplanted media use for these individuals. Finally, we will draw a political portrait. What are they like as political participants, and how does that picture compare with other online users?

A Demographic Portrait

Age

There is a clear generation gap when it comes to online discussion. Younger users (under thirty) are more likely than older people to visit newsgroups.[2] While three of five online users thirty and over were not on discussion forums, 55 percent of those under thirty were (see Table 3.1).

Moreover, they were online more often. While 31 percent of those under thirty said they were discussing at least weekly, only 25 percent of those sixty-five and older were discussing that often, and 17–18 percent of those between thirty and sixty-four.

People under thirty are overrepresented among online discussion users, compared with Internet users as a group. While 29 percent of those online are under thirty, 36 percent of online discussion participants are. The difference in age may be linked to the availability of time and Internet access. It takes time to read messages, follow threads, and post. Younger people particularly may have more time for such activity than others. They also

TABLE 3.1 The Online Discussion Generation Gap: Age Breakdown of Discussion Participants Compared with Other Online Users

Frequency of Online Discussion	Under 30 (%)	30–49 (%)	50–64 (%)	65+ (%)
Every day	7	5	5	5
3–5 days/week	11	6	4	7
1–2 days/week	12	7	7	13
Once every few weeks	12	8	8	7
Less often	13	15	11	10
Don't discuss	45	58	65	57
Total*	100	99**	100	99**
N =	576	975	332	110

* "Don't know" and "refuse" responses have been omitted.
** Rounding error.
Chi square significant at the .01 level.

Source: Pew Research Center for the People and the Press, January 14, 1999.

may be more likely to have someone else to talk to, since there are so many other young people on these groups. Younger people, particularly college students, often have free access to the Internet through educational institutions making them slightly more likely to go online.

There is another story here, however—that many people sixty-five and older have discovered online discussion. Although the number of those online is no greater than for younger age groups, the frequency of their participation in discussion is closer to that of those under thirty than those between thirty and sixty-four. One-fourth of online users over sixty-five said they were in discussion at least weekly, compared with 18 percent of those between thirty and forty-nine and 16 percent of those between fifty and sixty-four. Here too it may come down to time—the oldest online users may have more time than their younger cohorts. Once they are online, that time difference may allow them to participate in discussions more often.

Gender

Despite the existence of some female-dominated electronic discussion forums, overall electronic discussion has been viewed as a male bastion. Of those in online discussion, 57 percent were male. Among other online users, the majority (55 percent) were female. Male online users are drawn to electronic discussion, while most women online are not.

This gender gap is particularly true of Usenet. One study of Usenet political groups found they are clearly male-dominated, with 73 percent of posters being male and 75 percent of the messages coming from males. The study of twenty-seven groups also found that no group had more women than men, only one had equal numbers, and two had no women at all.[3]

There also may be differences in online behavior between male- and female-dominated groups. Flaming and profanity are more common in male-dominated than in female-dominated groups.[4] However, in male-dominated groups, posts from women are just as likely to flame as those from men. In our four groups, messages sent by females were nearly as likely to flame other posters. While 31 percent of messages sent by males included flames of other posters, 28 percent of messages sent by females did so.

Table 3.2 shows that the gender gap is pronounced even among those who are online discussants. Men are more likely than women to engage in online discussion frequently. While one-half of male online users said they discuss online at least some of the time, only 39 percent of women who were online said they did so. Moreover, men discuss slightly more frequently than women do. While 26 percent of men said they discuss at least weekly, 19 percent of women did.

TABLE 3.2 Gender Differences in Online Discussion Frequency

	Male (%)	Female (%)
Frequency of Online Discussion		
Every day	7	5
3–5 days/week	9	6
1–2 days/week	10	8
Once every few weeks	10	8
Less often	15	11
Don't discuss	50	61
Total	101*	99*
N =	499	605

* Rounding error.
Chi square significant at the .01 level.

Source: Pew Research Center for the People and the Press, January 14, 1999.

Other Demographic Differences

Marital Status   Marital status is a major dividing line between those who discuss and those who do not (see Table 3.3). Online discussants were less likely than other online users to be married and more likely to have never been married. Fifty-one percent of those in online discussion were married, compared with 61 percent of those who were not discussants. A larger proportion of online discussants have never married—37 percent versus 24 percent of those who are not in online discussion.

Moreover, the gap grows even larger as online discussion frequency increases. Less than half (47 percent) of the most frequent online participants were married.

Educational Background   At first glance, it would appear that both those who discuss and those who do not are well educated. Seventy-nine percent of those who do not participate have at least some college education, and 78 percent of those who do participate have at least some college education.

However, the differences appear when one looks at the level of college education. Those who participate tend to be less well educated than those who do not. Among those in online discussions, people with some college are the most populous group; among those not likely to participate, the largest group is college graduates.

While 50 percent of those not participating are at least college graduates, only 40 percent of those who are most active online are at least college graduates (see Table 3.3). Those who do not participate at all or do so very

TABLE 3.3 Other Demographic Differences

	Married (%)	College Graduate (%)	Still in School/ College (%)	Income Less than $50K (%)	Own Home (%)
Online discussants	51*	40*	29*	45*	59*
Nondiscussants**	61	50	20	37	67

* Chi square significant at the .01 level.
** Online users, but not participants in online discussion forums.

Source: Pew Research Center for the People and the Press, January 14, 1999.

infrequently are better-educated than those who discuss online at least once every few weeks. But those who participate a lot (every day) are better-educated than those who participate a moderate amount (weekly or several days a week).

These people who participate more often may be slightly more confident of their ability to participate. We may see the differences more starkly later when we compare posters and those who do not post. Yet the best-educated are more likely than those less educated not to be in online discussion. Perhaps they feel less of a need to participate in the forums. They may have other forums for expression, such as high-status occupations or involvement in social organizations, that those with only some college education may lack.

The difference may also be related to age again. It could well be that the lack of a college degree means they are still in college and have not yet graduated. In fact, 29 percent of discussants were still in school, compared with 20 percent of nondiscussants.

Income/Home Ownership   Online discussants are poorer than others who are online. Forty-five percent of online participants make less than $50,000 in annual income. Thirty-seven percent of others online are in that income category (see Table 3.3).

One more difference is in home ownership, which is generally a sign of permanency (see Table. 3.3). People who participate in online discussion are slightly less likely to own their own homes. While two-thirds of those who are not on discussion forums own their own home, 59 percent of those who are do so.

A Portrait of Computer Use

Online discussants are heavy computer users, and not just for work. For example, the vast majority of online discussants said they had used a

TABLE 3.4 Frequency of Online Discussion by Length of Time Online

Time Online	Every day (%)	3–5 days/ week (%)	1–2 days/ week (%)	Every few weeks (%)	Less often (%)
6 months	12	16	22	16	13
1 year	15	29	28	24	28
2–3 years	30	32	33	38	40
More than 3 years	44	24	17	21	19
Total*	101*	101*	100	99*	99*
N =	112	147	177	177	267

* Rounding error.

Source: Pew Research Center for the People and the Press, January 14, 1999.

personal computer at home yesterday, while only slightly more than one-half of other online users had done so.

They are also well acquainted with the Internet. The more frequently they are online as discussion participants, the more they are inclined to be Internet veterans (see Table 3.4). Those who participated every day were far more likely than even those who were online discussants several days a week to have been on the Internet for more than three years. While 41 percent of those who were online discussants less often than once every few weeks had been online one year or less, a whopping 44 percent of everyday users of online discussion had been on the Net more than two years.

Discussants are much more experienced at using the features of the Internet, such as audio and video clips. They were much more likely than nonparticipants to have viewed a video clip or listened to an audio clip. They also outpaced nonparticipants in the practice of bookmarking Internet sites.

Discussants also are well versed in e-mail. That is obvious for participants in e-mail discussion lists. Seventy-seven percent of the most frequent participants said they send or receive e-mail every day, while only one-third of those who did not participate in discussion received or sent e-mail that often.

Online Frequency and Activity

Online discussants were more frequent users of the Internet. Thirty-six percent of online discussants said they were online daily. Only twenty-seven percent of other online users were on that often (see Table 3.5).

The most frequent discussion participants also were heavy daily users of the Internet. A majority—59 percent—of those who never went to

TABLE 3.5 Differences in Online Behavior Between Discussion Participants and Nonparticipants

	Go online daily (%)	Go online for work/ pleasure (%)	WWW (%)	E-mailed family, friends (%)	Send/ receive e-mail daily (%)	Made an online buddy (%)
Online discussants	36*	68*	88*	68	38**	38*
Nondiscussants	27	55	81	68	32	10

* Chi square significant at .01 level.
** Chi square significant at the .05 level.

Source: Pew Research Center for the People and the Press, January 14, 1999.

discussion forums went on the Internet no more than once a day. And 40 percent of those who participated several days a week said they went online no more than once a day. However, only 24 percent of the most frequent participants said they went on the Internet that infrequently. Forty-six percent of that group said they went online three or more times each day.

The discussion likely encourages more frequent online usage. Usenet and e-mail participants go online frequently in order to track the discussion. Particularly if they post, they may want to see how people respond. This may even be true of chat rooms, though for a different reason. In chat rooms, individuals often make appointments to meet in certain rooms later in the day.

Participants in online discussion forums are less likely to go online strictly for work. They go online for a mixture of work and pleasure. Perhaps they go online for work but also use some of that time to participate in online discussion. Whereas, those who never participate are more likely just to use the Net for work (see Table 3.5).

Online discussants also were more likely than nondiscussants to be on the World Wide Web. They also were more likely to send and receive e-mail daily. Given their online sociality, it is not surprising that more than one-third had made a friend via online communication. Only one in ten nondiscussants had done so.

Attitudes Toward Going Online

But frequent participants also felt somewhat guilty about the amount of time they spend going online. While only 7 percent of those who never go to electronic discussion forums said they spend too much time online, 15 percent of those who participate several days a week and 24 percent of those who go online daily admitted they spend too much time on the Internet. Yet there is a strong attraction because the extent of participating is strongly linked to the amount of regret one would have if online access was no longer possible (see Table 3.6). Online discussants may be more involved with the Internet than those who do not discuss. For example, 55 percent said they would miss "a lot" going online if they could not do it anymore, while 39 percent of non-subscribers said they would miss the Internet that much.

The more frequent one's participation in online forums, the more one said online access would be missed "a lot." The most frequent participants were more than twice as likely as the nonparticipants to say they would miss their Internet life "a lot." Online discussion seems to create an allure that frequent participants feel somewhat guilty about but would be very reluctant to part with.

This may be due to discussants' usage of the Internet as a tool for expression and communication with others versus those who use the Internet as a means for information gathering from Web sites. They are somewhat more likely to use the Net for interpersonal communication.

Participation in online discussion also may affect how one thinks about information transmitted over the Internet and its effect on people. For example, online discussants felt that online communication was more a profitable development for human relationships than a harmful one. When asked whether the advantage of the Internet in allowing people to meet and stay in touch outweighed the disadvantage of increasing computer-mediated communication instead of face-to-face contact, online discussants were significantly more likely than nondiscussants to see the former as more important (see Table 3.6).

Online discussants may be less prone to see dangers with the Internet in other ways as well. For example, they were less worried than others online

TABLE 3.6 Differences in Online Attitudes Between Discussion Participants and Nonparticipants

	Would miss going online (%)	Agree that more communication on Internet is advantage (%)	Worry some or a lot about a computer virus (%)	Favor law to ban online pornography (%)
Discussants	55*	71*	46**	46*
Nondiscussants	39	63	40	54

* Chi square significant at .01 level.
** Chi square significant at .05 level.

Source: Pew Research Center for the People and the Press, January 14, 1999.

about the threats of computer viruses. They also tend to be less supportive of a government role on the Internet. For example, only 46 percent of those who discussed agreed that the government ought to make it illegal for a computer network to carry pornographic or adult material. However, 54 percent of nondiscussants felt that way.

Interaction with Others

The stereotype of an online discussion member might be a social isolate who cannot relate to people in real-world settings. However, in reality, online participants were no less likely than other online users to interact with others offline. As Table 3.5 shows, online discussants as a whole were no less likely than others to have e-mailed family or friends. And Table 3.7 reveals that the more frequent one's online discussion activity, the more likely an online discussant was to have called a friend or relative recently just to talk.

In fact, in some respects online discussion participation may reflect a need to have extensive social interaction, either online or offline. Those who are online discussants actually may be quite social individuals. Online discussion apparently supplements, but does not supplant, offline interpersonal activity. These social individuals have found a new way to communicate and discuss.

Perhaps the need of these individuals for social interaction is not adequately met by offline interaction. This may be more true of individuals who live alone, work from home, or spend long hours commuting, particularly alone in an automobile.

Portrait of a News Consumer

We might expect that online discussants use newsgroups as a substitute for other news sources, particularly since many are disdainful of regular news

TABLE 3.7 Call a Friend or Relative Just to Talk?

	Frequency of Online Discussion				
	Every day (%)	3–5 days/ week (%)	1–2 days/ week (%)	Once every few weeks (%)	Less often (%)
Yes	71	61	61	56	56
No	29	39	39	44	44
Totals	100	100	100	100	100
N =	112	147	176	178	267

Source: Pew Research Center for the People and the Press, January 14, 1999.

outlets. But online discussants are more frequent news consumers than are others who are online but are not part of the discussion community (see Table 3.8). Forty-six percent of those who discuss online say they go online for news every day. By contrast, only 31 percent of those who never discuss do so. They also search for political news more than other online users. One-half said they go online for political news, while a little more than a third of nondiscussants do so. Also, the more frequent their participation, the more likely they go online for news on politics. This may be a tool for online participants to keep informed in order to participate in online discussion.

They also are more likely to use the features of the Internet to gather news. Nearly one in four said they have customized pages that gives them updates of specific news topics they are interested in. Only 13 percent of nondiscussants had them.

Those who participated in electronic discussion were more likely than nonparticipants to have bookmarks to news media sites. Also, they had more news media site bookmarks: the former had an average of twelve sites bookmarked versus seven sites for nonparticipants. Moreover, they are more inclined to get news e-mailed to them on topics of interest. Online discussants were more prone to visit Web sites related to specific issues or policies of interest to them. Over one-third visited such sites, while only 22 percent of nondiscussants did so.

One example of use of the Internet for specific political news gathering was the reaction to the 1998 Clinton-Lewinsky scandal that resulted in the impeachment of President Bill Clinton. One-third of online discussants said they went online for news of the scandal, compared with 26 percent of those who never discussed online. Similarly, one-fourth went online to read Starr Report documents, compared with 18 percent of nondiscussants.

TABLE 3.8 Differences in Online Media Usage Between Discussants and Nondiscussants

	Go online for news at least weekly (%)	Go online for political news (%)	News e-mailed (%)	Custom news (%)	Book-mark media sites (%)	Visit issue sites (%)	Follow Lewinsky scandal (%)	Read Starr Report (%)
Online discussants	46*	50*	26*	23*	72*	36*	33*	25*
Nondiscussants	31	36	12*	13	55	22	26	18

* Chi square significant at the .01 level.

Source: Pew Research Center for the People and the Press, January 14, 1999.

Traditional Media Exposure

Some proponents of electronic discussion suggest that this new medium may be replacing traditional media.[5] People who use electronic discussion, it is argued, increasingly are abandoning their traditional news media habits in favor of forums such as Usenet, e-mail, and chat. If this is true, then we should expect to see a lower usage of the news media and more negative attitudes about the media among online discussants. If it is also true that the more one uses electronic discussion, the less one would use traditional news media, we should expect to see less media exposure among the most frequent participants.

Actually, we find this is not true. Online discussants are just as frequent traditional media users as those not discussing. Overall, participants have no less media exposure than other online users (see Table 3.9). They read newspapers only slightly less often than nonparticipants. However, it is difficult to know whether online newspaper sites are included. Since online discussants are more likely to bookmark news media sites, it is possible they are reading newspapers more often online than in print version.

However, they clearly use other traditional media slightly more often. They watch television news programs slightly more frequently than nonparticipants—66 percent versus 63 percent. They also are more likely to listen to radio news daily than are nonparticipants.

All of this shows that, despite claims to the contrary, online discussion does not displace media viewing or reading. Online discussants are no less likely to use traditional media. In fact, they may be slightly more likely to do so. Moreover, when combined with their more extensive use of online news sources, these electronic discussants were heavier news consumers than were slightly those not participating.

The supplemental, rather than supplantive, nature of online discussion is demonstrated in one Usenet poster's remark: "I do get the NYT [*New*

TABLE 3.9 Differences in Traditional Media Usage Between Discussants and Nondiscussants

	Read newspaper yesterday	Watched television news yesterday	Listened to radio news yesterday	More news exposure since going online
Online discussants	50	66**	52*	17
Nondiscussants	54	63	48	14

* Chi square significant at the .01 level.
** Chi square significant at the .05 level.

Source: Pew Research Center for the People and the Press, January 14, 1999.

York Times] every day, and the [Washington] Post and the Washington Times and the Wall Street Journal . . . and I still find usenet a valuable source of in-depth news reporting."[6] It is possible that online discussion actually may enhance traditional media use. Frequent discussion participants were slightly more likely to say they used traditional news sources more often than they had before going online.

Attitudes Toward Traditional Media

Given their slightly greater usage of traditional media, it could be assumed that online discussants' attitudes toward traditional media would be the same as those who do not discuss. Yet their attitudes toward the traditional media were more negative than others who are online. One-half of online discussants agreed with the statement: "These days you're more likely to find accurate information about what's going on in the world on the Internet than in the daily newspapers or on the network news." Forty percent of nondiscussants agreed with that statement.

Online discussants were more inclined than nondiscussants to consider information on Web sites of news organizations to be more accurate than information that the same news organizations had on their offline versions. The vast majority of both groups felt there was not a difference, but 16 percent of online discussants felt that way, compared with 9 percent of nondiscussants.

Online discussants obviously have doubts about the traditional media, even more so than other online users. However, those doubts do not seem to diminish their reliance on traditional media, since they use it no less often, and perhaps even slightly more so.

A Political Portrait

A critical question posed by this book is whether online discussants differ politically from other online users who do not discuss. We can answer that question by examining the differences between these two groups in levels of political interest, nature of political attitudes, extent of political participation, partisan tendencies, and voter preferences.

Level of Political Interest

Online discussants report that they are not more interested in government affairs than other online users. In fact, they are slightly less interested. Yet other measures would suggest that they equally or more interested. Online discussants follow politics because they enjoy politics more than those who are not in online discussions. Thirty-five percent of online discussion participants said they followed politics because they enjoyed it (as opposed to doing so as a duty), compared with 23 percent of nondiscussants who felt that way. As mentioned earlier, they were much more likely than non-participants to go to Web sites related to issues such as the environment, gun control, abortion, and health care reform. Online discussants were more inclined to go online to get election news. Twenty percent of online discussants did so, compared with 13 percent of other online users.

Trust

Do online discussants think about politics differently than those who do not discuss online? Mainly, no. However, one difference is the issue of trust. Characteristics of online discussion such as the relative anonymity of the setting (even when a name and e-mail address are provided) and the level of flaming might suggest that electronic discussants are less trusting of others. Indeed, they are, slightly. While 46 percent of online users felt you "can't be too careful" in dealing with other people, 52 percent of online discussants agreed with that statement.

However, there is an interesting caveat: the more frequently one discussed online, the lower the percentage agreeing with that statement. Those who discussed frequently were more trusting of others than those who discussed infrequently. The most regular participants were not more suspicious of others, as might be predicted. On another measure of trust, online discussants also were not less trusting of government than others who were not in online discussions. On still another attitude indicator—satisfaction with the country—they also did not differ significantly from nondiscussants.

Political Participation

Though their levels of trust are not much different from other online users, there are distinctions in political participation (see Table 3.10)

TABLE 3.10 Differences in Political Behavior Between Discussants and Nondiscussants

	Registered to vote (%)	Vote turnout (%)	Contacted or e-mailed officials or organizations (%)
Online discussants	77*	58	19*
Nondiscussants	83	66	12

* Chi square significant at .01 level.

Online discussants are more active in e-mailing public officials or groups about public policy or political issues than those who are not discussants. The more frequent one's participation in online discussion, the more likely one had sent an e-mail to a political official or organization on a political issue. Only 12 percent of nondiscussants said they had e-mailed a political official or organization. However, 19 percent of discussants had. The greater level of discussion, the more one had e-mailed. For instance, 34 percent of those who discussed daily had sent a political e-mail.

Offline political participation by discussants was lower than for other online users. A smaller proportion of online discussants were registered to vote—77 percent compared to 83 percent of nondiscussants. The lowest level of voter registration was found among those who discussed the most often: only 73 percent of those discussing daily were registered to vote. And online discussants were slightly less likely than others online to actually vote. While 66 percent of other online users voted in 1998, only 58 percent of online discussants went to the polls.

The explanation probably lies not so much with the tendency to discuss or not discuss as with their occupational status and lack of permanent residency. Remember that nearly three in ten online discussants said they were still in college. The lower levels of political participation may be attributable to their youth and college status.

Partisanship and Vote Preference

Given the predominance of conservative thought on forums such as Usenet, one might expect online discussants to identify primarily with the Republican Party. However, as Table 3.11 shows, that was not the case. Fewer online discussants than nondiscussants considered themselves Republicans. However, the trend was not toward the Democratic Party. Although slightly more discussants than nondiscussants considered themselves Democrats, and Democrats actually slightly outnumbered Republicans among online discussants, an important difference between the two groups was the independent category. Online discussants were less likely to affiliate with either political party.

That independent streak did not manifest itself as strongly in vote choice in 1996. Table 3.12 reveals online discussants to have been more supportive of Clinton than Dole in 1996. Only 8 percent of online discussants gave their vote to Ross Perot, a percentage similar to that of nondiscussants, while 7 percent voted for a candidate other than Clinton, Dole, or Perot. Again, that figure was similar to the voting among nondiscussants.

TABLE 3.11 Party Differences Between Online Discussants and Nondiscussants

Party affiliation	Online discussants (%)	Nondiscussants (%)
Republican	28	34
Democrat	29	27
Independent	31	27
No preference	8	8
Other	1	1
Don't know/refused	4	4
Total	101*	101*
N =	1,104	881

* Rounding error.

TABLE 3.12 Vote Choice Differences Between Online Discussants and Nondiscussants

	Online discussants (%)	Nondiscussants (%)
1996		
Dole	29	34
Clinton	56	51
Perot	8	8
Other	7	6
Total	100	99*
N =	727	526
1998		
Republican	44	49
Democrat	47	44
Other/independent	9	7
Total	100	100
N =	359	513

* Rounding error.

Source: Pew Research Center for the People and the Press, January 14, 1999.

Differences Between Discussants and Others Online

Online discussants are significantly different from other online users on a number of measures. After reviewing what we know about online partici-pants, it is easy to disagree with the following description of electronic discussants: "The untamed, freewheeling nature of cyberspace means that it's often filled with every skinhead, Trekkie, religious zealot, and [Rush] Limbaugh-wannabe with a new theory on how the world should work."[7]

Demographically, compared with other online users not in discussions, discussants are younger, more likely to be male, less likely to be married, less well educated (though perhaps because they are still in college), and more likely not to own a home. Also, they are online sophisticates. They have more experience being online than others online. They readily use e-mail, audio, video, and bookmarks.

Unlike the prediction, they appear to be extensive consumers of news. Discussion supplements their news consumption. Moreover, despite negative attitudes about traditional media, they are no less frequent consumers of traditional news. Plus their use of online news means they may be much more frequent news consumers than others who are also online.

Politically, online participants appeared less likely to be partisans, less likely to be registered to vote, and less prone to actually turn out to vote than others who are on the Internet. Yet they are not predominantly Republicans, as might be expected. In fact, their tendencies were stronger than others online toward Democratic Party candidates.

But we have been treating online discussants as a monolith. In fact, they consist of two distinct groups—those who post and those who do not. What we will see next is how different these two groups of online discussants are even from each other.

CHAPTER 4

Posters Versus Lurkers

The online discussion is divided into two groups: those who speak out and those who do not. As we will see, the differences between these two can be stark and mark even more the distinctiveness of those who participate in online political discussion.

Posters are the visible members of the online community. Obviously the agenda and substance of online discussion revolve around them. Their interests and opinions are viewed as the sum total of online discussion content.

However, there is another group: people who follow the discussion but do not say anything, commonly called lurkers. Usage of the term, which connotes stealth and a desire for anonymity, expresses some negative implications attached to the practice by the online discussion community. The habit of following a conversation but not saying anything, or in many cases not making one's presence known, suggests a sense of voyeurism.

Lurkers are largely anonymous on newsgroups. They are not so anonymous on e-mail lists since the list manager knows who they are. But they are almost always unknown to others on the electronic mailing list. Anonymity also exists to some extent on chat, where the names of individuals in the session are available to all others on the chat channel. Yet since the names typically are screen names or nicknames, the actual identity of the individual is not compromised.

How Many Lurkers?

The question of how many people lurk rather than post is important because it helps determine the size of the online community. Using the number of posters alone may be only the tip of the iceberg. But this question is often difficult to answer, particularly in the case of Usenet. Estimates of the number of lurkers have varied. As mentioned earlier, one group of scholars estimates that there is one message posted by an individual for every ten messages read.[1] That might suggest a rough estimate of the ratio of posters to lurkers of 1:10. Or, according to another study—this time of a listserv—found that less than one-third of subscribers actually posted messages.[2] Thus the ratio of posters to lurkers may be much less, say 1:3. That figure suggests a much smaller online discussion number of lurkers.

According to the Pew Center survey, the number of lurkers actually was somewhere between those two estimates. Lurkers constituted three-fourths of those who participate in online discussions. That means posters are a small minority of the online discussion population.

Listserv participants are slightly less likely to lurk. Twenty-eight percent of those on listservs said they had expressed an opinion about a social or political issue on an online forum, and over one-fourth of those had done so in the past week. Their greater tendency to post may be a function of their active effort to subscribe to and therefore join a list. It also may relate to the more specialized and exclusive nature of such lists. There may be less fear that one will be flamed among a more intimate group or that posting may attract annoying spammers, as is often the case with posting in chat rooms or newsgroups. More e-mail list participants actually post, but they may do it less often than those in Usenet or chat.

Why Lurk?

Why do people lurk in the first place? Why don't they express themselves online like posters do? It is important to note that, for many people, lurking may be a temporary phenomenon—something they do until they become familiar with the medium. As Table 4.1 shows, the more frequently one participates, the more likely one will post messages and not just lurk. Forty-nine percent of those who participated every day said they had posted. Moreover, that frequency of participation seems to be a threshold. Under that level of frequency, less than one-third of participants are posters.

Of course, posting also may increase frequency of participation. The very act of posting may involve the individual more intensely in the discussion and enhance frequency of participation. As one becomes

TABLE 4.1 Posting Versus Lurking by Frequency of Online Discussion

	Every day (%)	3–5 days/ week (%)	1–2 days/ week (%)	Every few weeks (%)	Less often (%)
Posters	49	30	21	20	14
Lurkers	51	70	79	80	86

Chi square significant at the .01 level.

absorbed in a particular thread, participation may rise as the poster goes to online forums repeatedly to see whether anyone has responded to his or her message and to determine how the thread is progressing.

Yet Table 4.1 also reveals that one-half of even the most frequent participants still had not posted. These people may be the most committed lurkers.

Lurkers may become posters when they finally become animated enough about a thread to want to participate. One post on a Usenet group started: "Boy, I almost never reply to newsgroups, and I was against impeachment, but THIS post is RIDICULOUS!!! I don't think I have a choice but to respond!!!"

Unfortunately, we do not know enough about why more lurkers do not become posters. We can speculate that lurkers may be analogous to individuals in offline conversations who do not say very much. These could be similar to individuals in a small group who remain silent while others talk, students in a class who never ask a question, participants in a town meeting who do not speak out, or even a majority of Americans (once termed "the silent majority" by Richard Nixon) who are aware of current events but make no public statements or actions about them. Such individuals choose not to be vocal, particularly on matters of politics. However, their participation in online discussions, even as silent members, suggests an interest in the discourse and a willingness to serve as audience for those who do express their opinions.

Lurkers also may be afraid of the reaction to a post. One possible reaction would be neglect, that is, no one responds. The message meets with a dead silence and the individual's attempt to initiate a thread or respond to a thread is ignored. Another possible reaction relates to flaming. Lurkers worry that their post may be attacked by others for a variety of reasons—not germane to the list, wrongheaded, not thoughtful enough, or whatever.

Lurkers are generally ignored by posters, particularly since posters usually do not know who they are. Unlike in a face-to-face small-group conversation, where someone is very likely to notice an individual who has said nothing, online discussants largely are oblivious to the presence of others.

There are exceptions. A list manager on a listserv could encourage an individual subscriber to participate in a discussion thread. In a chat channel, particularly when few individuals are present, other participants can encourage a particular individual who is present but has not spoken to contribute something to the discussion. But for the most part, lurkers constitute an unseen audience posters are vaguely aware of but rarely seek to include.

The Contrasts

Since the online community includes both posters and lurkers, it is necessary to include both in an analysis of that community. Obviously, there is one cardinal difference between the two groups—posters register their views online, while lurkers do not. But is that all? Or are there other differences between the two groups?

Such questions are not insignificant. The posters, due to their vocal role, become the representatives of the entire online community. But what if the posters' representation of the online community is not an entirely accurate one? Perhaps posters cannot speak for lurkers as well because they do not typify them as well. Let's compare posters and lurkers to see whether they are more alike than different.

Demographic Differences

Age Though young people clearly are overrepresented in discussion forums, as seen in the previous chapter, they are only slightly more likely to be posters than lurkers (see Table 4.2). Posters are slightly younger than lurkers. The mean age for posters was thirty-five, compared with thirty-eight for lurkers. On the other end of the age spectrum, senior citizens tended to be underrepresented. The posters, then, seem to represent the younger participants in the online community. What appears in electronic talk is slightly more likely to be reflective of the interests of those among the younger participants in online discussion.

Gender Posting and lurking separate men and women. Posters are far more likely to be men than women. Thirty-six percent of posters were women. That compares with 45 percent of lurkers who were female. Twenty-seven percent of men said they had posted, compared with one in five females.

TABLE 4.2 Posters and Lurkers Compared by Age

	Posters (%)	Lurkers (%)
Under 30	38	35
30–49	43	47
50–64	17	12
65+	2	6
Total	100	100
N =	153	56

Source: Pew Research Center for the People and the Press, January 14, 1999.

In the four Usenet groups we selected for study, discussed in Chapter 2, male dominance was apparent. Only 7 percent of the posters were female. (Those without clearly identifiable names could not be coded by gender. Additionally, it is possible that an online name doesn't reflect the poster's gender.) The percentage of female posters ranged from a high of 11 percent on alt.politics.radical-left to 2 percent on alt.politics.usa.constitution (see Table 4.3). Female posters were even slightly less represented in terms of posting. Overall, only one in twelve messages posted came from female posters. The most male dominated group was alt.politics.usa.constitution, where only 1.3 percent of the messages were from females.

The level of participation by women according to the Pew survey is much lower than that of men. Over half (54 percent) of women reported they had posted a message only once. Nearly two-thirds (63 percent) of male posters had posted multiple messages.

What we see online in the form of postings, e-mail messages, or chat messages primarily will be the thoughts of males. Women more likely will be the ones listening rather than posting. Therefore, the male dominance in electronic communities is magnified in the actual discussion.

Marital Status/Dependent Children   We might assume that those who are vocal participants in electronic political talk are people using this medium to communicate with others. Perhaps they are the segment of the online community that is single. Indeed, that was true. While a bare majority—52 percent—of lurkers were married, only a minority of posters (46 percent) were married. Posters were more likely than lurkers to have never married. Forty-four percent of posters were single, compared to one-third of lurkers. They also were less likely to have dependent children living in the home with them (see Table 4.4).

TABLE 4.3 Gender Representation of Posters in Selected Usenet Groups

	Clinton (%)	Constitution (%)	Radical-Left (%)	Republican (%)
Male	92	98	89	95
Female	8	2	11	5
	100	100	100	100
N =	138	48	91	131

TABLE 4.4 Other Demographic Differences Between Posters and Lurkers

	Married (%)	No dependent children (%)	College graduate (%)	Still in school/ college (%)	Income less than 50K (%)	Own home (%)
Posters	46	70	43	31	47	56
Lurkers	52	58	39	28	44	60

Source: Pew Research Center for the People and the Press, January 14, 1999.

The lifestyle of active participation online may be more likely to downplay other obligations—marriage and/or child care. Or that lifestyle may be the product of a single status and no dependent children. Individuals actually may be using online discussion to reach out for contact with other people, albeit in the artificial and controlled environment of online discussion.

Education   We might assume that posters are better-educated since they feel comfortable expressing themselves online and feel they can articulate their views in front of a mass audience. Perhaps they are more likely than lurkers to be college-educated. In fact, they are better educated, but only slightly. A larger percentage of posters than lurkers are college graduates. The significant difference may be among the less well educated. (However, remember that the online community generally is well educated.) While 15 percent of posters had a high school diploma or less, 24 percent of lurkers had that educational level. The less well educated who visit online discussions may feel more reticent about expressing opinions online.

Other Demographic Differences   There were no significant differences between posters and lurkers in other demographic areas. Posters were slightly more likely to be college students, have a lower income, and not own a home. This would correspond with their youth as well, as noted above.

Computer and Online Usage

As we established in the last chapter, online discussants are quite computer-savvy. But is there even a difference among posters and lurkers? One might expect that since posting and frequency of participating in online discussion are related, as shown in Table 4.1, posters would be the more computer-savvy of the two groups.

That is true. Posters and lurkers differ significantly in their online experience and use. For example, posters have much more tenure online than lurkers. Seventy percent of posters had been online for two or more years, compared with 56 percent of lurkers (see Table 4.5).

Posters also spend much more time online than lurkers (see Table 4.6). Fifty-three percent of posters said they go online every day. Only three of ten lurkers said they were online that often. Seventeen percent of lurkers said they went on as infrequently as less than once a week. Only 7 percent of posters were online that rarely.

TABLE 4.5 Length of Time Online: Posters and Lurkers Compared*

	Posters (%)	Lurkers (%)
Length of time online		
6 months	9	18
1 year	21	27
2–3 years	36	36
More than 3 years	34	20
Total	100	101**

* Chi square significant at the .01 level.
** Rounding error.
Source: Pew Research Center for the People and the Press, January 14, 1999.

TABLE 4.6 Differences in Online Behavior Between Discussion Participants and Nonparticipants

	Online daily	Go online 2 or more times	Online work/ pleasure	On WWW	E-mailed family, friends	Send/ receive an e-mail daily	Made online buddy
Posters	53*	64*	73*	95**	76**	62*	62*
Lurkers	30	46	66	86	65	46	31

* Chi square significant at the .01 level.
** Chi square significant at the .05 level.

Source: Pew Research Center for the People and the Press, January 14, 1999.

Nearly two-thirds of posters said that on an average day they go online two or more times. However, less than half of lurkers went online that often. Those who post also are more likely than lurkers to use the Internet for both work and pleasure.

Posters use the Internet to communicate more with others than lurkers do. They are more likely to send or receive e-mail or send e-mail to family or friends on a daily basis. Additionally, far more posters have made an online buddy of someone they have never met in person.

Posters have more online savvy than lurkers. They are more likely to use bookmarks. Seventy-seven percent of posters had bookmarks, while 60 percent of lurkers had bookmarks. They also have more familiarity with the multimedia components of the Web. Seventy-six percent of posters had listened to an audio clip over the Web, compared to 54 percent of lurkers. Seventy-two percent of posters had watched a Web video clip, while only 52 percent of lurkers had done so.

Posters and lurkers also differ in knowledge of computers and the Internet. Four of five posters correctly identified Microsoft as the computer software company involved in an antitrust dispute with the government. That compares with 69 percent of the lurkers. Posters and lurkers also differ in their comprehension of Internet lingo. Forty-four percent of posters knew what *org* in a Web site address meant, while only 31 percent of lurkers did.

Attitudes About Going Online If posters and lurkers differ in online behavior, perhaps they also contrast on their attitudes about the Internet. Given that posters have been online longer, go online more often, and are more frequent participants in online discussion, one might expect that posters are more positive about their online experience.

However, the differences between the two were not as stark as expected. Attitudes about going online did contrast between posters and lurkers on some issues, but they were similar on others. Far more posters than lurkers said they would miss "a lot" going online if they could not do it anymore (see Table 4.7). More than three-fifths said they felt that way, while only two-fifths of lurkers agreed with that statement.

Posters and lurkers were similar in their attitudes that the advantages of more communication on the Internet outweighed the disadvantages of less face-to-face communication. They also had similar feelings about computer viruses. But they both differed significantly on the issue of whether one would find more accurate information on the Net than in daily newspapers or on network news. They also diverged on the issue of whether online pornography should be banned. Posters were less supportive of such a ban.

TABLE 4.7 Differences in Online Attitudes Between Posters and Lurkers

	Would miss going online a lot	Agree that more communication on Internet is advantage	Worry some/ a lot about a computer virus	More accurate information on Net	Favor law to ban online pornography
Posters	64*	73	46	55**	38*
Lurkers	41	70	46	48	49

* Chi square significant at .01 level.
** Chi square significant at .05 level.

Interaction with Others   Given their propensity to express their views, and our findings from the last chapter that online discussants are offline socialites as well, we might expect that posters are more social and talkative offline as well. Indeed, posters were slightly more social. Seventy-six percent of posters said they had visited with family or friends yesterday, while 68 percent of lurkers had done that. Sixty-three percent of posters said they had called a friend or relative the day before just to talk. Fifty-nine percent of lurkers said they had done that.

Online Media Differences   Do posters and lurkers differ in terms of their online news consumption? They do. Posters are far more likely than lurkers to go online regularly for news of current events. As Table 4.8 demonstrates, more than two-thirds of posters said they went online for news at least weekly. But less than one-half of lurkers did so.

They also outpace lurkers in terms of interest in going online for political news. Three of four posters went to the Net for political news, while only two-fifths of lurkers were online for political news.

The two groups diverge markedly as well in using the Internet to specialize news gathering. Forty-three percent of posters said they had news e-mailed to them on specific news topics of interest to them. Only one in five lurkers used such a service. Similarly, one-third of posters had a customized page online that gave them updates on specific news topics matching their interests. Again, only one-fifth of lurkers had such a page. A third innovation, book-marking news media sites, was more popular among lurkers—68 percent said they had such a bookmark. However, bookmarks were more popular among posters; four of five had one.

Political information on the Web seemed to interest posters more than lurkers. Nearly three of five posters said they visit Web sites where they can gather information about specific issues or policies. But only three of ten lurkers went to such sites.

The major political event of 1998—the Clinton/Lewinsky scandal—was an opportunity for many posters to follow online news reports, but not so

TABLE 4.8 Differences in Online Media Usage: Posters and Lurkers Compared

	Go online for news at least weekly	Go online for political news	Had news e-mailed	Custom news	Bookmark media sites	Visit issue sites	Follow Lewinsky scandal	Read Starr Report
Posters	68*	75*	43*	33*	81*	57*	51*	40*
Lurkers	43	41	21	19	68	30	27	20

* Chi square significant at the .01 level.

Source: Pew Research Center for the People and the Press, January 14, 1999.

much for lurkers. A majority of posters said they went online to get news about the scandal, but only 27 percent of lurkers said they had done so. The Starr Report was read online by 40 percent of posters but by only 20 percent of lurkers.

Traditional Media Use

The contrasts in online media usage might suggest the same incongruities in traditional media. However, posters and lurkers are remarkably similar in their traditional media usage. Table 4.9 shows that posters are not leaving the traditional media. One-half of posters are still reading a newspaper and listening to radio news daily, and two-thirds say they watch television news daily. Even those who are most involved with Internet discussion are not using it as a means for displacing other sources of news.

Politically Different?

We have reviewed some significant differences between posters and lurkers demographically and in terms of media usage. But are they different politically? This question is critical because a significant contrast between posters and the rest of the online discussion community may mean that the political messages emanating from discussion do not even represent the electronic political discussion community, not to mention the larger population.

Level of Political Interest First, we can compare these two groups in their level of political interest. Given posters' willingness to express themselves and their more intense usage of news media for information, it seems a safe guess that they are more politically interested than lurkers. Posters do indeed follow politics much more frequently than lurkers. Table 4.10 presents the finding that while less than half of lurkers said they follow government and public affairs most of the time, 30 percent of posters said they did so. Posters clearly have a stronger desire to know what is going on

TABLE 4.9 Traditional Media Usage: Posters and Lurkers Compared

	Read newspaper yesterday (%)	Watched television news yesterday (%)	Listened to radio news yesterday (%)	More news exposure since going online (%)
Posters	47	66	49	19
Lurkers	50	67	50	15

Source: Pew Research Center for the People and the Press, January 14, 1999.

TABLE 4.10 Frequency of Following Politics: Posters and Lurkers Compared

	Posters (%)	Lurkers (%)
Most of the time	60	46
Some of the time	25	31
Only now and then	9	14
Hardly at all	6	9
Total	99*	100
N =	207	672

* Rounding error.
Chi square significant at the .05 level.

Source: Pew Research Center for the People and the Press, January 14, 1999.

politically than do posters. But these findings also show that posters are atypical—that is, more like political junkies—even when compared to others in the online discussant community.

Political Attitudes However, there is not much difference between posters and lurkers in political attitudes. The only significant difference was in trust of others. Lurkers tended to be less trusting of other people. Lurkers also were slightly more prone to be satisfied with the country's direction (see Table 4.11).

Level of Political Activity There were some significant differences in political activity between the members of the two groups. As Table 4.12 shows, four-fifths of posters were registered to vote, compared with three-fourths of lurkers. Two-thirds of posters said they had voted in the last election (1998), while just more than half of lurkers (55 percent) said they had

TABLE 4.11 Differences in Political Attitudes: Posters and Lurkers Compared

	Satisfied with country's direction	Trust Washington only some/ never	Can't be too careful in dealing with people %
Posters	52%	74%*	47*
Lurkers	58	70	53

* Chi square significant at .01 level.

Source: Pew Research Center for the People and the Press, January 14, 1999.

TABLE 4.12 Differences in Political Behavior: Posters and Lurkers Compared

	Registered (%)	Voted 1998 (%)	Contacted or e-mailed officials or organizations (%)
Posters	81	66*	51**
Lurkers	75	55	10

* Chi square significant at .05 level.
** Chi square significant at .01 level.

Source: Pew Research Center for the People and the Press, January 14, 1999.

voted. There was a dramatic difference in efforts to affect policy. One of every two posters said they had contacted or e-mailed public officials or groups about public policy. Only one of ten lurkers had done that.

Posters clearly are more active politically than lurkers. The contrast in attempting to contact officials shows the stark distinction between the politically involved posters and the less active lurkers.

Partisanship and Vote Preference Posters and lurkers were somewhat different in party affiliation (see Table 4.13). More posters than lurkers identified themselves as Republicans: one-third of posters, compared with just over one-fourth of lurkers. Lurkers were somewhat more prone to self-identify as Democrats.

Lurkers and posters differed as well in vote choice (see Table 4.14). Lurkers were far more likely to support Clinton in 1996. Nearly three-fifths of lurkers voted for Clinton, compared with one-half of posters. They also were less inclined to vote for candidates other than those of the three main parties.

TABLE 4.13 Party Affiliation: Posters and Lurkers Compared

	Posters (%)	Lurkers (%)
Party ID		
Republican	33	26
Democrat	25	30
Independent	33	30
No preference	7	9
Don't know/refused	2	4
Total	100	99*

* "Other" omitted.

Source: Pew Research Center for the People and the Press, January 14, 1999.

TABLE 4.14 1996 Presidential and 1998 Congressional Vote Choice: Posters and Lurkers Compared

	Posters (%)	Lurkers (%)
1996		
Dole	31	28
Clinton	50	59
Perot	10	7
Other	9	5
Total	100	99*
1998		
Republican	46	41
Democrat	41	40
Other/independent	7	7
Don't know/refused	6	12
Total	100	100

* Rounding error.

Source: Pew Research Center for the People and the Press, January 14, 1999.

Separate Communities

Posters and lurkers both share an interest in online discussion forums. They frequent the same forums—newsgroups, listservs, or chat. They follow the same threads and read the same posts. But the two groups are different in significant ways. Posters are slightly younger. A majority of both posters and lurkers are male, but the majority is significantly larger among posters. Females are less likely to be visible in the online community. Posters are more likely than lurkers not to be married and not to have ever married. It is less likely that a poster's home includes children under eighteen. They are also slightly better-educated.

The demographic profile of a poster, then, may be a young, college-educated male who is unmarried. The lurker is also likely to be a male, but a bit less so than for the poster. The lurker is married and likely has dependent children at home. The lurker is slightly less likely to be college-educated and is slightly older.

The differences between the two groups are starker when we examine their online experience. Posters are online sophisticates compared to lurkers. They have been online longer. They spend more time online. They are more knowledgeable about computers and the Internet. They avail themselves of numerous online features. They send and receive e-mail more often.

Posters' attitudes about the Net differ somewhat from those of lurkers. Posters are more likely to miss going online if they could not do it anymore. They put more stock in online information than in the traditional news media. They also oppose a government role in regulating the Internet, particularly pornography. Posters are more wedded to their computers and to the online experience than are lurkers both in attitude and behavior.

Politically, there are substantial differences between posters and lurkers. Posters tend to be more interested in politics, more likely to be registered voters, and more likely to actually turn out to vote. They also affiliate with the Republican Party more than lurkers do, and consequently were less likely than lurkers to vote for Bill Clinton in 1996 and more likely to vote for a Republican congressional candidate in the 1998 midterm elections.

Our analysis of these two groups reveals some substantial differences between them that may impact our ability to say that posters are representative of the online discussion community. Their demographic differences, particularly on gender, their greater online sophistication, and their political activism suggest that in many ways they are different from their silent partners in online discussion. The more conservative tone of online political discussion may be attributable not to a conservative online discussion community but to a vocal minority who are more ideologically conservative than their silent counterparts.

Does this matter? If online discussion content becomes a gauge for public will, it is important to note that it may not even be an accurate gauge for the online discussion community. What we see on our computer screens during online discussions is not a representative sample of those who are part of the online discussion community. It is a distortion tilted in favor of the younger segments of the community who are male, who have embraced the Internet, and who are politically interested and politically active.

But even if online discussants are not representative of the online community, perhaps they still are emblematic of the broader general public. That is our next subject.

CHAPTER 5

Virtual Representation

When we use online political discussion as a gauge of public opinion, we make a fundamental assumption: that the content of online discussion somehow mirrors the public's opinions. But can we make that assumption? Are online posters or lurkers representative of the rest of us?

One way to determine whether they are is to compare online discussants and the public. We can do this using two measures: discussants' similarity to the public in terms of demographic background and political attitudes and behavior, and correspondence between the issue interests of online discussants and the general public.

Demographics

If we were to paint a demographic portrait of posters, would they "look like America" or would they look different? Let's compare the two groups and see.

Age

As Table 5.1 shows, the online community does not reflect America in terms of age. Clearly, posters and lurkers are much younger than the general public. Over one-third of posters and lurkers are under thirty, while only 22 percent of the general public are that young. At the other end of the age spectrum, citizens over sixty-five are underrepresented. Seventeen

TABLE 5.1 Age, Gender, and Marital Status: Posters, Lurkers, and the General Public Compared

	Posters (%)	Lurkers (%)	General Public (%)
Age			
Under 30	38	35	22
30–49	43	47	42
50–64	17	12	19
65+	2	6	17
Total	100	100	100
Gender			
Female	36	45	52
Marital Status			
Married	46	52	53
Divorced	0	2	13
Never married	44	34	21

Source for posters and lurkers: Pew Center for the People and the Press, "The Internet News Audience Goes Ordinary," January 14, 1999, at http://www.people-press.org/tech98que.htm.

Source for general public data: Census Bureau estimates, July 1, 1998 (under 30 includes 18 to 29).

Question wording: "Are you married now and living with your husband/wife or are you widowed, divorced, separated, or have you never married?" (results for last two options not shown).

percent of the general public are over sixty-five, but only 6 percent of lurkers and, amazingly, only one of fifty posters are over sixty-five.

The age discrepancy is due partly to the embrace of computers and the Internet. Those under thirty are the age group most likely to be online in the first place.

So what difference does this make? Senior citizens' views are nearly absent. The policy agenda is heavily skewed toward a young population. Using online discussion messages as a gauge of public opinion clearly can result in a severe age bias, threatening to ignore the political attitudes of a significant segment of the population.

Gender

As mentioned earlier, electronic political discussion appears to be the domain of males. They dominated in the political groups studied as well. More broadly, males constitute nearly two-thirds of all posters and more than one-half of the lurkers. Table 5.1 demonstrates how significant that is when compared with the general population. While 52 percent of adults are female, the electronic discussion community is primarily male, with the vocal element of that community strongly male-dominated.

As with age, the problem with taking online discussion as representative of the concerns of the larger population may be the deemphasis on issues important to groups underrepresented in the online discussant community. In this case, it would be women. Women's issues, such as child care, health care, and education, receive minimal attention in groups, particularly compared to other issues such as gun control, crime/violence, and foreign policy, as shown in Chapter 1. The product of this distortion may be the assumption that such issues carry little weight with citizens. Political leaders and journalists may misread the public's interests by relying on online discussion as an assessment of public opinion.

Marital Status

Posters were less likely than the general population to be married. They also were more likely to have never married. Over 40 percent of posters had never married, compared with one-fifth of the general population. To a large extent, this is probably a function of age. As we have already established, posters tend to be younger and more likely to be still in college. But it also suggests a reason posters may be more involved on the Internet: they may not be living with family members, particularly a spouse.

Does this matter? Possibly. Posters may be less concerned about issues of importance to Americans who are married, particularly those with children, since many are themselves still young and single. Message traffic may address less often issues such as education of children, the mortgage tax deduction, property taxes, and the like.

Education

Both posters and lurkers differ significantly from the general population in educational level (see Table 5.2). While 43 percent of the general public have never been to college, 73 percent of lurkers and 80 percent of posters hold college degrees. Online participants are well educated, a point we noted earlier. But this comparison reveals how much better educated they are than the public generally.

As a consequence, postings need to be viewed as the opinions of a well-educated minority rather than of a cross section of the general public. Those who are not college-educated—nearly one-half of American

TABLE 5.2 Educational Level: Posters, Lurkers, and the General Public Compared

Level	Posters (%)	Lurkers (%)	General Public (%)
8 grades or less	0	0	5
9–11 grades	3	3	9
High school diploma or equivalent	12	20	30
12 yrs+ w/no higher degree	3	2	20
Junior/community college degree	37	34	9
BA-level degrees	24	25	17
Advanced degree incl. LL.B.	20	14	11
Don't know/refused	0	1	0
Total	99*	99*	101*
N =	209	672	1281

* Rounding error.

Question wording: "What is the highest degree you have earned?"
Source for posters and lurkers: Pew Center for the People and the Press, "The Internet News Audience Goes Ordinary," January 14, 1999, at http://www.people-press.org/tech98que.htm. t

adults—may find their views not represented online, since very few people in that category post. Since these voices are often underrepresented in American politics, their weakness in this setting is additionally disturbing.

Income

Since online discussants are significantly younger than the general population, it might be safe to assume they are less affluent. But that is not the case. As Table 5.3 illustrates, posters and lurkers actually enjoy higher income than the general population. Thirty-two percent of the general public make less than $20,000. However, only 12 percent of posters and 10 percent of lurkers are in that income category. The one-tenth or so of the online community who are at the lowest income level may well be in that category only because they are college students temporarily at the low end of the income spectrum. The dragging down of the income levels by these college students suggest that other posters may be even more affluent than these numbers indicate.

At the other end of the income scale, 12 percent of the general public have an annual income of $75,000 or more, while 20 percent of lurkers and 22 percent of posters are at that income level. A majority of posters and lurkers make over $40,000 annually; however, a majority of the general population make under $40,000.

TABLE 5.3 Income Level, Home Ownership, College Student Status: Posters, Lurkers, and General Public Compared

Income Level	Posters (%)	Lurkers (%)	General Public (%)
Less than $10,000	4	3	14
$10,000–$19,999	8	7	14
$20,000–$29,000	12	10	13
$30,000–$39,999	12	13	11
$40,000–$49,000	12	11	12
$50,000–$74,999	17	20	16
$75,000–$99,999	11	10	8
$100,000+	11	10	8
Don't know/refused	14	16	0
Totals	101*	100	100
Home Ownership			
Own home	56	60	66
Rent	37	28	32
College student status			
In college	31	28	7

* Rounding error.

Question wording: "Does your family own your home, pay rent, or what?" Results of third option omitted.

Source for posters and lurkers: Pew Center for the People and the Press, "The Internet News Audience Goes Ordinary," January 14, 1999, at http://www.people-press.org/tech98que.htm.

The online community represents an economically affluent group and is not an accurate sample of the various economic levels within the U.S. population. Citizens with low incomes are grossly underrepresented in the online community. Even those with middle-level incomes are underrepresented.

The income disparity between the online discussants and the general public seriously calls into question the representativeness of this group vis-à-vis the general public. Using the online discussion community as a standard of general public opinion is like using people who live in affluent parts of a metropolitan area as representative of all the citizens of that city.

Home Ownership

Home ownership is widely considered the American dream. Two-thirds of American adults own their own home. Owning a home can be linked with stability and increase in likelihood of political involvement, particularly voter turnout.[1] The affluence of these online political discussants might predict they would be homeowners, perhaps more so than the average American adult.

However, that is not true. Probably in accordance with their single status and youth, posters are much less likely than the general public to be homeowners (see Table 5.3). This discrepancy in home ownership probably can be attributed to the youth and college status of so many posters. Again, they are young, and many are still college students. But the same problem of representativeness emerges as with preceding measures such as marital status, age, gender, and income: issues of concern to homeowners are likely to be ignored or downplayed.

Still in College

The preceding chapter showed that nearly one-third of posters and over one-fourth of lurkers are college students. Table 5.3 reveals how overrepresented college students are in the online discussion community versus the general population. According to the U.S. Census Bureau, only 7 percent of adults fifteen and over are currently in college. Obviously, the online community varies markedly from the general public in occupation. A significant minority are still college students worrying about grades, rather than workers who hold full-time jobs.

Although academics sometimes use college students as representatives of the general public in experiments and surveys, the folly of equating college students with the general public in terms of representativeness is apparent to most people. They no more serve as an accurate representation of the general public than would any other particular occupational segment such as computer programmers, farmers, or taxi drivers. In many ways, due to their age and educational background, they may actually be much less representative.

Media Use

Posters and lurkers are frequent consumers of news, as we discovered in the preceding two chapters. But how does that compare with the general public? As Table 5.4 shows, online discussion community members actually are similar to the general public in media use habits. Levels of newspaper reading are similar for posters, lurkers, and the general public. A little less than half of the general public said they read a newspaper yesterday. That is very similar to the newspaper reading habits of posters and lurkers. Television news viewing also was quite similar. All three

TABLE 5.4 Daily Newspaper Reading, Television News Viewing, and Radio News Listening: Posters, Lurkers, and General Public Compared

Read Daily	Posters (%)	Lurkers (%)	General Public (%)
Yes	47	50	47
No	53	50	53
Watched News			
Yes	66	67	65
No	34	33	35
Listened to News			
Yes	49	50	41
No	49	49	57
Don't know	2	1	2
Totals	100	100	101
N =	209	672	1,201

Question wordings: "Did you get a chance to read a daily newspaper yesterday, or not?" "Did you watch the news or a news program on television yesterday, or not?" "About how much time, if any did you spend listening to any news on the radio yesterday or didn't you happen to listen to the news on the radio yesterday?" (with Pew data collapsing times into "yes, listened" and "no, did not listen").
Source for all data: Pew Center for the People and the Press, "The Internet News Audience Goes Ordinary," January 14, 1999, at http://www.people-press.org/tech98que.htm.

groups had the same proportion of individuals who had viewed television news yesterday—approximately two-thirds.

Only radio news use was dissimilar. Online discussants were somewhat more likely to listen to radio news than was the general public. The difference may stem from the young age demographic of the online discussion community. Young people between the ages of 18–25 spend more time listening to music on the radio than those who are older. Therefore, they would pick up radio news and information from that listening. Another reason may be online discussants' interest in supplementing their traditional media exposure with talk radio listening.

Politics: Interest, Attitudes, Behavior

Since political opinions are expressed constantly in online discussion, and those outside sometimes monitor such expressions, the political attitudes of online discussants in comparison with the general public is an important next step in measuring representativeness. Are discussants more politically interested and active than the general public? Given their presence on online political discussion forums, one would assume so. But how much more interested and active are they? That is the question.

Follow Politics

Not surprisingly, posters and lurkers are much more likely to follow politics than are ordinary citizens (see Table 5.5). Posters particularly are very unlike the general public in their levels of political interest. Three-fifths of posters said they follow government and public affairs most of the time. However, most of the general public (60 percent) follows politics some of the time or now and then. Lurkers are in between but closer to the posters than the general public. Nearly one-half of lurkers said they follow politics most of the time, while less than one in three say they do so "now and then" or "hardly at all." But over one-third of the general public say they follow politics that infrequently.

This finding suggests that posters and lurkers are extremely atypical in their attention to politics. They are probably more passionate about political issues than the general public. Consequently, their attitudes reflect those of a small minority of political sophisticates rather than the general public. It would be more accurate to call them representative of a group of activists rather than of the general public. As we will see later, this attention to politics affects their political behavior, making them distinctive from the general public in that respect as well.

Another measure of political interest is the pursuit of political information. We have learned that both online discussants and the general public use traditional media similarly. But what about online discussants' use of online information? Are online discussants more prone to seek out election information from online news sources? The answer is yes and no, as Table 5.5 also shows. While two of five posters went online in 1998 for election information, only one in seven lurkers did so. Surprisingly, lurkers were less likely to go online for election information than the general public. A significant difference, then, between at least posters and the general public is the process of supplementing, in that posters rely more frequently on online news sources.

We concluded in the previous chapter that traditional news media habits have not been altered for the posters and lurkers; instead, they have been supplemented by the Internet. But the vast majority of those

TABLE 5.5 Frequency of Following Politics and Going Online for Election Information: Posters, Lurkers, and General Public Compared

	Posters (%)	Lurkers (%)	General Public (%)
Frequency of following politics			
Most of the time	60	46	28
Some of the time	24	31	37
Now and then	9	14	24
Hardly at all	6*	9	11
Go online for election information			
Yes	41	14	27
No	59	86	77

* Rounding error.

Following politics—question wording for all: "Some people seem to follow what's going on in government and public affairs most of the time whether there's an election or not. Others aren't that interested. Would you say you follow what's going on in government and public affairs most of the time, some of the time, only now and then, or hardly at all?"

Go online for election information—question wording for posters and lurkers: "Have you gone online to get news or information about the 1998 elections?"

Question wording for general public: "Did you see any information about this election campaign on the Internet/Web?" The question wording could have elicited varying responses from the two sets of respondents. However, one might expect that any bias due to question wording would have increased the general public's affirmative responses because the question asked not whether they had gone online to get information but merely whether they had seen it. The latter could have been the result of a serendipitous discovery. Therefore, in contrast with the posters and lurkers, the general public's numbers may be slightly inflated.

Source for posters and lurkers: Pew Center for the People and the Press, "The Internet News Audience Goes Ordinary," January 14, 1999, at http://www.people-press.org/tech98que.htm.

Source for general public data: National Election Studies, 1998.

in the general public have not been supplemented. They are still acquiring news primarily from traditional media and have not yet embraced online news as well.

As a result, posters (although not necessarily lurkers) are getting more news than the general public because they are not dropping their traditional news habits even as they embrace new online news habits. The news consumption pie for these individuals has grown; it has not been rearranged, and it has not shrunken.

Attitudes

The rhetoric that is common in political online forums might lead one to believe that the online discussion community is filled primarily with people who are highly dissatisfied with the U.S. government. Yet, as we saw earlier, that is not necessarily true. But how do posters and lurkers compare with the general public? Are they similar to the public in their levels of satisfaction with the country's direction or their levels of trust in government?

The answer clearly is yes. As Table 5.6 shows, posters and the general public were similar in their level of satisfaction with the direction of the country. Lurkers were even more satisfied than either posters or the general public. In fact, fewer posters, and far fewer lurkers, were likely to say they were dissatisfied with the country's direction.

Another measure of political attitudes is the level of trust—both in others and in the federal government. Are online discussants less likely to trust other people than the general public? One could assume so. Perhaps they engage in online interaction because they dislike interpersonal interaction in the real world. However, we have already learned that this is not necessarily so: online discussants are not social isolates who have little real-world contact with other people. Posters are even more trusting of others than are lurkers. But how do they compare with average citizens?

As Table 5.7 demonstrates, posters also are slightly more trusting than the general population as well. Less than one-half of posters agreed with

TABLE 5.6 Satisfaction with Country's Direction: Posters, Lurkers, and General Public Compared

Satisfaction	Posters (%)	Lurkers (%)	General Public (%)
Satisfied	52	58	50
Dissatisfied	41	35	48
No opinion	20	39	2
Totals	100	100	100
N =	200	672	1,005

Question wording: "All in all, would you say that you are satisfied or dissatisfied with the way things are going in this country today?"
Source for posters and lurkers: Pew Center for the People and the Press, "The Internet News Audience Goes Ordinary," January 14, 1999, at http://www.people-press.org/tech98que.htm.
Source for general public data: Gallup News Service, "Public Trust in Federal Government Remains High," January 8, 1999, at http://www.gallup.com/poll/releases/pr990108.asp.

TABLE 5.7 Trust in Others and Trust in Government: Posters, Lurkers, and General Public Compared

	Posters (%)	Lurkers (%)	General Public (%)
Level of trust in others			
Most people can be trusted	46	42	41
Can't be too careful	47	53	57
Other/depends	5	5	1
Don't know/refused	3	0	1
Trust in government			
Just about always	3	3	4
Most of the time	22	26	36
Only sometimes	67	62	58
Never	7	8	1
Don't know/refused	1	1	1

Trust in others—question wording: "Generally speaking, would you say that most people can be trusted or that you can't be too careful in dealing with people?"
Trust in government—question wording for posters and lurkers: "How much of the time do you trust the government in Washington to do the right thing?"
Question wording for the general public: "How much of the time do you think you can trust the government in Washington to do what is right—just about always, most of the time or only some of the time?"
Source for posters and lurkers: Pew Center for the People and the Press, "The Internet News Audience Goes Ordinary," January 14, 1999, at http://www.people-press.org/tech98que.htm.
Source for general public data: National Election Studies, 1998.

the statement that you "can't be too careful" in dealing with other people. More than one-half of lurkers and the general public agreed with that statement.

Given the fact that posters place their views out in the public and are not antisocial, this finding should not be a surprise. They may be more open with others, perhaps even more trusting than those in the general public. They appear to be more politically efficacious and perhaps more likely to believe they could capably handle interactions with others.

However, trust in government is a different story. These figures do conform to what we have seen in the rhetoric about government that is typed online every day. Those in the general public were far more trusting of the federal government than the online community (see Table 5.7). While 40 percent of the public said they trust the federal government at least most of the time, less than a third of lurkers and one-fourth of posters felt similarly. More than seven of ten online discussants said government could be trusted only some of the time or none of the time, while 60 percent of the public expressed that sentiment.

This lack of trust in government may be related to the conservative, antigovernment tone of electronic political discussion generally. Their postings are reflective of their antigovernment sentiments, as measured here. Online discussants may tend to differentiate between others, whom they trust, and government, which they seem more likely to distrust.

Political Behavior

Online discussants' higher levels of political interest should predict that they are more politically active than the general public. Indeed, it does, but not as much as one might expect. Posters are only slightly more likely than the general public to say they are registered to vote. While 78 percent of the general population said they were registered to vote, 81 percent of posters said they were. This distinction between the general public and online discussants probably also can be attributed to the latter's membership in demographic groups more prone to vote, such as the more affluent and the better-educated.

Most posters actually may be much more prone to vote than these figures indicate. As we have noted before, more than one-third of posters said they were still in college. College students typically have the lowest turnout among all age groups. Admittedly, these particular students may be different. But if their voting patterns match or at least closely resemble those of their peers, then their voter registration and turnout patterns would be lower than is indicated in Table 5.8. That may mean that the rest of the posters are almost universally registered voters.

TABLE 5.8 Voting: Posters, Lurkers, and General Public Compared

	Posters (%)	Lurkers (%)	General Public (%)
Registered to vote	81	75	78
Voted in last election*	66	55	52

* 1998 midterm election.

Voter registration —source for all data: Pew Center for the People and the Press, "The Internet News Audience Goes Ordinary," January 14, 1999, at http://www.people-press.org/tech98que.htm.

Vote turnout—source for posters and lurkers: Pew Center for the People and the Press, "The Internet News Audience Goes Ordinary," January 14, 1999, at http://www.people-press.org/tech98que.htm.

Vote turnout—source for general public data: National Election Studies, 1998.

Actual voting also differentiates the online discussion community, particularly posters, from the general public. As Table 5.8 also shows, posters were much more likely to be voters than were lurkers or the general public. In turn, lurkers were slightly more likely to have voted than the general public.

It must be noted that these figures are inflated because they represent self-reporting of voting, and survey respondents tend to overestimate their voting behavior. For example, the percentage of voters who participated in the 1998 midterm elections was 36 percent.[2] Even so, these numbers do suggest that posters and lurkers are voters more often than the general public. Again, this is particularly true for posters.

These findings confirm once again that posters are not typical Americans. They are much more politically active than their fellow citizens. They make ideal targets for candidate appeals because the vast majority will end up at the polls. But they are hardly representative of the general public.

Party Affiliation

Party affiliation is still another discrepancy between the online discussion community and the general public. Lurkers are more like the general public in partisanship, although fewer consider themselves Democrats and more express no party preference.

Posters clearly are distinctive. While 34 percent of the general public consider themselves Democrats, only one of four posters and three in ten lurkers identified as Democrats (see Table 5.9). Posters were slightly more likely than those in the general public to consider themselves Republicans. Thirty-two percent of posters called themselves Republicans, compared with 29 percent of the general public.

The slight advantage for Republicans among online posters is expected, in fact perhaps even more so than is indicated, but the dearth of Democrats, as compared with the general public, is a significant point. Again, this finding shows some incongruity between the general public and the online discussion community, particularly posters. These numbers should raise red flags about representativeness. They also help explain why the message content in electronic political discussion is weighted toward conservatives and against liberals. The sheer numerical disadvantage of Democrats in online discussion means they may be out-shouted online.

The finding concerning nonidentifiers is important as well. Both posters and lurkers were more inclined than the general public to say they are neither Republicans nor Democrats, nor even independents. This may be a

TABLE 5.9 Party Affiliation: Posters, Lurkers, and General Public Compared

Party	Posters (%)	Lurkers (%)	General Public (%)
Republican	32	26	29
Democrat	2	30	34
Independent	33	30	37
No preference	7	9	0
Other	1	0	0
Don't know/refused		4	0
Totals	100	100	100
N =	209	672	10,000+

Question wording: "Generally speaking, do you consider yourself a Republican, a Democrat, or an independent?"
Source for posters and lurkers: Pew Center for the People and the Press, "The Internet News Audience Goes Ordinary," January 14, 1999, at http://www.people-press.org/tech98que.htm.
Source for general public data: Gallup News Service, "Independents Rank as Largest U.S. Political Group," April 9, 1999, at http://www.gallup.com/poll/releases/pr990409c.asp.

minority who eschew partisan politics altogether. It also may reflect the heavy concentration of college students in the online community.

Vote Choice

A critical question is how online discussants vote as compared to the general public. Did their Republican partisanship translate into support for Republican candidates? Surprisingly, the answer is yes, but also no. As Table 5.10 shows, posters were much more likely to be supporters of Republican candidates for Congress in the 1998 elections than was the general public, which was essentially divided between the two parties. Lurkers matched the division within the general public.

However, the 1996 presidential election was a different story. That election found posters and lurkers abandoning the Republican candidate. Bob Dole received the support of only three in ten posters and even fewer lurkers. Clinton, however, was supported by one-half of posters and nearly 60 percent of lurkers.

The explanation may rest with the large proportion of the online community who are young college students. Dole was not popular among young voters.

TABLE 5.10 1996 Presidential and 1998 Congressional Vote Choice: Posters, Lurkers, and General Public Compared

	Posters (%)	Lurkers (%)	General Public (%)
1996			
Dole	31	28	4
Clinton	50	59	49
Perot	10	7	9
Other	9	5	1
Total	100	9*	100
1998			
Republican	46	49	49
Democrat	41	40	48
Other/independent	7	7	3
Don't know/refused	6	12	0
Total	100	100	100

* Rounding error.

Source for posters and lurkers: Pew Center for the People and the Press, "The Internet News Audience Goes Ordinary," January 14, 1999, at http://www.people-press.org/tech98que.htm; includes only those posters and lurkers who reported having voted

Source for general public data—1996 figures: Rhodes Cook, "Clinton's Easy Second-Term Win Riddles GOP Electoral Map," *CQ Weekly Report,* November 9, 1996, 3189–94.

Source for general public data—1998 figures: "How Recent Elections Compare," *National Journal,* November 7, 1998, 2667, and Richard M. Scammon, Alice V. McGillivray, and Rhodes Cook, *America Votes 23: A Handbook of Contemporary American Election Statistics* (Washington, D.C.: CQ Press, 1998).

Issue Interests

One question we raised earlier concerned the intersection of the issue agendas of the online community and the general public. Is online discussion representative in terms of issue concerns? Can we use the agenda of online discussion in order to gauge the issue concerns of the general public? If we can, we achieve another mechanism for recording public will. Moreover, such a method enjoys the advantage of easy accessibility (anyone can read online discussion forums) as well as immediacy (reaction to events occurs within hours).

However, as Table 5.11 shows, the issue agendas of Usenet posters in these four groups and those of the general public differed significantly.

TABLE 5.11 Issue Agendas: Usenet Posters and General Public Compared

	Clinton	Constitution	Radical Left	Republican	General Public
		% of threads addressing specific topic			
Education	0	0	0	1	17
Crime/violence	0	0	21	2	16
Taxes	2	0	0	1	15
Health care	1	0	0	1	13
Social security	2	0	0	0	10
Gun control	11	20	14	11	9
Economy	1	10	0	2	7
Budget deficit	0	0	0	1	6
Foreign policy	1	0	7	6	5
Drugs	0	0	0	1	5
Welfare	0	0	0	1	4
Defense	0	0	0	1	4
Ethics in government	4	0	0	4	4
Abortion	3	0	0	2	4
Medicare	0	0	0	1	3
Homelessness	1	0	0	1	3
Environment	0	0	0	3	2
Impeachment	11	0	0	1	2
Religion	0	20	0	3	2
Peace/nuclear arms	5	0	0	3	1
Civil rights	0	0	0	1	1
Immigration	0	0	0	4	1
Race relations	4	0	7	1	0
Terrorism	3	0	0	1	0
Other	50	50	50	46	4
Total	99*	100	99*	99*	

* Rounding error.

Source for Usenet group data: See Appendix.

Source of general public data: Harris Survey, September 17–21, 1999, question: "What do you think are the two most important issues for the government to address?" General public column does not add up to 100 percent because respondents were allowed to choose two important issues to mention, not just one. Also, the replies were "spontaneous and unprompted."

While the general public was concerned about education, crime/violence, taxes, and health care, the Usenet discussion focused around other topics, as discussed in Chapter 2. This study demonstrates that the interests of the general public do not seem to be accurately reflected in the agendas under discussion in electronic talk forums.

Electronic political discussion can be a very poor guide to what is important to the general public. Using electronic discussion as a gauge, one might conclude that education, crime, taxes, and health care were unimportant issues since they are discussed so little on these groups. Conversely, one might concluded that gun control was a highly salient issue for the public given the fact that it was the issue topic most consistently discussed across groups.

Journalists, politicians, and the general public need to beware of reading too much into the discussions that occur online. The potential for misreading the public's issue concerns is enormous when these electronic discussions are employed as measures of public opinion.

Representative or Not?

What do these data tell us about online discussants? They answer a fundamental question: can we use the online political discussion community as representative of the general public? The answer is clearly negative. Both posters and lurkers are dissimilar from the general public in key areas. Lurkers look more like the general public than posters by several indicators. However, posters clearly are distinctive demographically from the general public.

Simply put, the political postings of the online discussion community are those of individuals who look little like the general public. Compared with the general population, they are much better educated, more affluent, less likely to be married, and less prone to own a home. Significantly, they are much younger than the general public and more likely to still be in college. This conclusion is especially accurate when discussing posters.

In terms of political attitudes, posters are more distrustful of government than other citizens, although it should be noted that they are more trusting of other people. Moreover, posters' level of political interest is significantly higher than that of the general public. That high plane of political interest predicts their political behavior. Posters are more likely to register to vote. They also are more likely than their fellow citizens to actually vote. Their partisanship is unlike that of other voters. We don't know how strongly partisan they are, but we do know that they more frequently identify with Republicans than with Democrats, even though the general public is the opposite.

Finally, their partisanship seems to affect voter choice. The 1996 election results showed that posters, and particularly lurkers, may have been heavily influenced by candidate appeal (or the lack of it). However, when candidate appeal is minimized, as in a midterm congressional election, posters are drawn back to their partisan roots.

This analysis shows us that lurkers in many ways are more typical of average American voters, particularly in political attitudes and behavior, though demographically they are somewhat different. But posters—the voices of the online discussion community—are atypical. They do not look like other citizens. Nor, in most cases, do they think or behave politically like them.

CHAPTER **6**

Conclusion

This book started with a question: can online political discussion represent public opinion in the eyes of political leaders, candidates, journalists, and others who seek understanding of the public's will? The question was hardly a moot one. The ease of using this medium, coupled with its apparent populist structure and the claims of some of its advocates, suggested its ability to serve in such a role.

But this analysis of both those who constitute the online community and its content confirms that it would fail in that role. Those who post differ substantially from the general public on several measures. They represent far more the young, well-educated, and affluent rather than the public as a whole. Given the skew of the online discussion community, it is no surprise that their issue interests also vary from those of the general public.

The failure of electronic talk is particularly disappointing given the promise of such a medium as a democratic and participatory forum. The reach of the medium, the ability to focus attention on specific issues and the seemingly unlimited span of discussion topics suggest that electronic talk possesses significant potential as a political deliberation tool. Yet, as presently constituted, it is fraught with obstacles to its use as a forum for the determination of public opinion. In fact, as Chapter 2 suggests, given the characteristics of discussion—exclusion of others, flaming, a great deal of anonymity—it is even problematic as a public discussion forum. These barriers lessen its ability to serve the political system.

Why does electronic political talk fail? A related and perhaps more important question is what, if anything, can be done in order to fit this medium for such a function. Let's answer the first question and thereby possibly work toward a response to the second.

Basically, the problems with electronic political discussion can be divided into two broad categories: the environment for participation and the unrepresentative nature of the current participants. Each of these leads to the medium's inability to serve a deliberative function. Let's take each of these in turn.

Environment

The milieu of potential political discussion shapes the form of that discussion. For example, Nina Eliasoph argues that people avoid discussing politics in public settings, though they discuss politics privately. They do this, she contends, because of a lack of social acceptability for discussing politics in most settings. Bluntly, we discourage people from discussing politics in public settings. The problem Eliasoph identifies is the dearth of appropriate settings. Speaking of people she studied, she concluded there were "too few contexts in which they could openly discuss their discontent."[1]

On its face, electronic political talk offers an environment where political discussion is not only acceptable but expected. Yet on deeper examination of this forum, we have seen that the environment mitigates against full political discussion. The problems stem from the absence of the following critical components: a moderating role, accountability, and an attitude of engagement.

Lack of Moderating Role

For most online discussions there is no moderator. This is particularly true for newsgroups and chat rooms. The existence of freewheeling discussion actually is considered by many online discussants to be a virtue. They enjoy the ability to say what they think without any check by a monitor.

However, the lack of a moderating role also severely inhibits discussion and particularly deliberation. No one is there to lead the discussion in constructive directions or exercise authority over participants who break the social rules for discussion. Even if an individual poster attempted to play such a moderating role, the probable response would be repudiation and ridicule.

Unmoderated discussion lends itself to chaos. As political scientists Pippa Norris and David Jones note, "Virtual democracy looks more like anarchy than ABC News."[2] The absence of a moderating role results in a haphazard agenda-setting process. The agenda-setting role is played by a small group of unrepresentative posters. Essentially, the group's agenda can be set by anyone who wants to do so and who has the time to spend online. There is no polling of individual participants or consensus on what constitutes worthy topics for discussion.

Overall, there is a lack of rules or any mechanism for their enforcement. Anyone can form a group. Anyone can participate in a group. Anyone can say anything he or she wants and attempt to take the discussion wherever he or she wishes it to go. As long as someone is persistent and has allies (or followers), that person can dominate the discussion.

A moderator also could elevate the tone of the discussion by moving it beyond accusation or polemics. Rarely do posters support their positions through rational argument and supporting evidence. In fact, when other posters challenge them, they too often rely on ad hominem attacks. By contrast, a moderator might challenge posters to use rational argument to defend their positions or at least eschew ad hominem references.

The lack of a moderator also means the absence of any emphasis on actual problem solving or resolution. To those who seek to dominate the agenda, expression is more important than resolution of problems. With the exception of those who enjoy ranting, there is frustration over the pointlessness of such online encounters. Some basic questions should be asked: "Is the group constantly pushing out people who really belong? Are members leaving because they find the group unproductive or unsatisfying?"[3]

Lack of Accountability

The environment of these political forums also fails to create a sense of accountability on the part of participants. The approach to online political discussion too often is one of participating without having to be called to account to anyone for what one says or does online. Usenet groups and chat rooms are perfect examples of such behavior. Individuals come and go without explanation or warning. There is no connection with a particular group.

Yet primary groups, such as families, neighborhoods, and community organizations, are essential ingredients if Americans are to move from faceless masses to participating individuals.[4] They offer an environment in which people can express themselves, but also a realization that those expressions affect ongoing social relationships.

The Internet is supposed to duplicate that by offering a virtual community peopled by virtual citizens and even virtual friends, but there is genuine concern that the Net actually displaces real community. Robert Putnam admits his hunch that "meeting in an electronic forum is not the equivalent of meeting in a bowling alley."[5] Indeed, it is not.

The Web is not a virtual political community; it is a collection of geographically disparate, isolated individuals. The frequent inability of discussion participants to give human characteristics to those with whom one is conversing can lead to a dismissal of the existence of human elements in message recipients. Since others are never seen, heard, or touched, they cannot convey nonverbal messages that communicate humanness.

These signals can be significant indications of social acceptance or rejection. However, virtual communities exist without them. When someone misbehaves in a real community, there are social consequences: interpersonal ostracism leading to temporary withdrawal of human interaction.

However, online communities are not capable of doing the same. Admittedly, an individual can be ostracized: replies to discussion threads are not written, or condemnation of the individual is broadcast to the group. However, within seconds, the individual easily can join another online community. One faces no discernible social consequences for bad behavior.

This lack of accountability contributes to the attitude of calumny toward others, which produces extensive flaming. Such flaming is less common in a real community because face-to-face interaction often precludes that level of conflict. Most individuals are more conflict-averse when they are physically in the presence of others. A lack of accountability does not merely lead to flaming. It can also reduce the willingness to participate in the discussion. Excitement about participation likely diminishes as individuals face the prospect of personal attacks from others.

Flaming is a perpetual problem for political online discussion. Posters freely attack one another. For example, in the wake of contentious verbal clashes on an AOL-sponsored newsgroup, the AOL monitor pleaded with posters to "make this a more amiable place where any person, regardless of faction, can openly discuss political issues and current events."[6]

The lack of civility makes for an inhospitable environment for many potential posters. Such behavior is hardly unique to explicitly political groups. One study of a less explicitly political Usenet group found that "the arguments begin to lose any rational basis and the debate is often reduced to a series of harangues and name-calling that express deep antagonisms."[7] But the fact that this lack of civility is common among political talk potentially makes rational discussion the exception rather than the rule.

The Absence of Engagement

The basic premise of any political blog, newsgroup, chat room, or mailing list discussion is furnishing a platform where individuals can engage in political discussion. One study of online discussion participants concluded participants enjoy going online to converse with others who have different views.[8]

However, the content of online discussion suggests engagement is exactly the ingredient so often missing from that outlet. One cause of this shortage of actual engagement is the structure of electronic discussion. Online talk segregates participants into a multitude of narrowly specialized discussion groups. This is not unique to online political talk. The Internet, generally, produces severe audience fragmentation, as Cass Sunstein has pointed out.[9]

People gravitate to other like-minded people on mailing lists, in chat rooms, and in newsgroups. This lack of engagement is most pronounced on mailing lists, where people purposely find niches where they can avoid contact with opposing viewpoints. Obviously a structure that overtly excludes people who do not conform to the opinions of the group aids reinforcement, but it hampers opinion exchange.

As a result, electronic talk participants are too frequently set in their own discussion ghettoes: liberals in one corner, conservatives in another. One poster even admitted as much in a post: "I don't want to discuss these things with you. It's pointless. I just am interested in stating my position. You state yours. End of discussion." Even when participants do interact, they too often talk past one another without enough listening to others, particularly those with whom they disagree. John M. Streck has concluded that "[c]yberspace, in other words, on a day to day basis is about as interactive as a shouting match."[10]

On political groups, discussion threads often are not discussions but monologues. Individuals start a thread with some provocative statement and then respondents chime in with their own opinions. But actual dialogue among participants is less frequent. In fact, sometimes posters openly confess they cannot achieve dialogue with others since their opponents are beyond reasoning with.

One contributing factor to the scarcity of discourse is the practice of cross-posting, particularly on Usenet. The political newsgroup message too often appears to be a blast across Usenet rather than an attempt to interact with others. The individual poster seems less interested in engagement than in pronouncement. Opinions are set. The goal clearly is expression and reinforcement, not interaction and exchange.

As mentioned earlier, adding to this problem is the growing number of organizations placing press releases on seemingly sympathetic newsgroups or listservs. The groups view these efforts as free advertising. However, they add to the clutter of online discussion and debase the capability to engage in online interaction.

A related development is the increasing adoption of online political discussion for pushing particular interests, including commercialization. Press releases by various organizations and corporations appear as posts and attempt to draw discussion participants to the Web address of the sender. Additionally, groups are using online discussion forums as mass mailing tools. Commercialism is spreading on Usenet as new companies are organizing to place commercial ads on Usenet groups and link commercially oriented sites link to newsgroups.[11]

However, the effect of this trend on discussion is as inhibiting as if someone at a dinner party began repeating a commercial instead of engaging in discussion. Such efforts again suggest that Usenet and e-mail discussion lists are becoming more like free commercial bulletin boards than discussion forums.

The absence of engagement applies not only to those who actually post but also to those who do not. Lurkers essentially become voyeurs in the conversation. They can observe the conversation without participating, without actually engaging in interaction. Much like political discussions offline, they are the majority that merely spectate. Admittedly, many people do that in social conversations. However, online interaction is a simple process, not any more complex or time-consuming, for those who are already lurking in discussions. Yet engagement is limited to a select few of the online community, while the majority merely spectate and thereby weaken the medium's participatory promise. This lack of involvement in the discussion by these individuals, especially when they can easily do so, suggests that many who potentially could participate are failing to become players in the process of political discussion.

Unrepresentative Nature of Participants

As noted in the preceding chapter, electronic political talk participants do not represent a cross section of American life. Online discussants vary significantly from the general public demographically and in terms of media usage, political interest, political attitudes, and behavior. Succinctly, online participants are more like political activists than ordinary citizens.

The importance of this point about unrepresentativeness hinges on the uses to which electronic discussion is put. If it is employed as an indicator of public opinion, then it misleads through distortion. The reflected public opinion, as indicated by the posters, is the viewpoint of an affluent, well-educated, highly politically interested, and conservative majority of the population.

If, on the other hand, online political discussion is viewed by politicians, journalists, and the public as a microphone for a certain portion of the population to express itself, then the distortion is erased. Such a usage limits the applicability of online discussion. It also robs the medium of its promise as a yardstick of public will.

However, the very existence of online discussion tends to lead to its employment as a reflection of public sentiment. It becomes an easy and quick mechanism to register public mood. Public reaction to events can be recorded within hours or even minutes at low cost. There is no need to wait for public opinion surveys. A news story about reaction can be written; a response to an event can be recorded; conclusions about public opinion can be drawn. But such conclusions could be inaccurate due to the unrepresentativeness of those who may be called upon to serve as the representatives of the public.

Online political discussion lacks representativeness. The online community is quite incongruous with the larger American citizenry according to a variety of measures. Moreover, those who are most active participants online—the posters—are the least representative. In other words, those who set the agenda, carry the discussion, and serve as the gauge of public opinion are most unlike the public they supposedly would be a likeness of.

The unrepresentative nature of those who speak the loudest in American politics—letter writers, campaign contributors, activists—is nothing new. However, reliance on these online discussants as representative, despite optimistic rhetoric to the contrary, is similarly flawed.

Not a Deliberative Body

The failures of online political talk as a forum for political discussion can also be applied to its function as a forum for political deliberation. In fact, in some regards, online political arenas are less well equipped to be deliberative forums than those existing offline. Computer-mediated communication possesses certain traits that hinder the decision-making process: it can take longer to reach consensus, the outcomes can be less related to the individual aims of the participants, and the discussion can feature the expression of extreme viewpoints.[13]

One drawback, as noted above, is the anonymous nature of online interaction. Charles White outlines the differences between online political discussion and democratic deliberation: "[D]eliberation is a public act, in which opinions must be advanced and defended in the full light of public scrutiny, not in the shadows of electronic anonymity."[14] Yet relative (if not near total) anonymity is a staple of online discussion, one that many current online discussants probably would be loath to part with.

Still another limitation is the unrepresentative nature of participation. As stated above and in the preceding chapter, these participants do not serve as accurate gauges of public will. Moreover, the current operation of electronic political discussion militates against future involvement by broader sections of the public, despite a potential willingness to do so as increasing numbers of Americans go online.

The flaws in the current usage of electronic political talk would suggest its inability to assist a democratic political system. What then? Should the potential of Internet technology be abandoned due to the current defective structure? At present, the answer is yes. But perhaps there is hope. Is it possible to create another forum in which online political discussion can take place? Is there still an opportunity to create electronic public space that serves democratic functions?

The Ideal Public Space

Our second question at the beginning of this chapter, and the more compelling one, was: what must be done in order to reshape this medium to function as a public deliberative forum in a democratic society? This question turns our attention to whether it is possible to design the ideal electronic public space.

The concept of a public sphere has been a popular ideal for a coterie of communications scholars. But what is a public sphere or space? What does it look like? How does it work? Definitions vary, but they have common elements. Jürgen Habermas defined public space as a sphere of private people coming together as a public.[15] Nina Eliasoph called the public sphere "the realm of institutions in which private citizens can carry on free and egalitarian conversation, often about issues of common concern, possibly welding themselves into a cohesive body and a potent political force."[16]

Public space is a place where individuals can express themselves as members of a polity and find common ground and even consensus for political action. It is a sphere of respect and appreciation for contrasting views. But it is not limited to a mechanism for expression. It is a vehicle for public deliberation and problem solving.

Public space has become a desirable but elusive ideal. In fact, some scholars have argued that it has become an even more implausible concept over time. Habermas has bemoaned the demise of a public sphere in social and political life.[17] For example, the physical structure of cities has limited the existence of public space. Modern urban design does not create "free space for public contacts and communications that could bring private people together to form a public."[18]

According to Habermas, the existence of such a space is a prerequisite of democracy since the fundamental rights of individuals to exercise political power are connected to its very existence.[19] Eliasoph argues that public space actually generates political power among citizens.[20] However, the effort to create such space seems futile. Instead, modern trends of commercial malls and shopping centers have displaced town squares and common areas as public settings for political discussion and deliberation.

Yet the emergence of interactive communications has reinvigorated the search for public space. New ideas to create public space employing communications technology have emerged in recent years. In 1984, Benjamin R. Barber suggested creation of a Civic Communications Cooperative with the objective of integrating interactive broadcast technology into a public deliberative process.[21]

Since the mass availability of the Internet, the discussion has taken still another twist. The potential for this technology to serve such a function as a deliberative tool is greater than for any other in the past. Accordingly, the calls for creation of electronic public space via the Internet have grown in number and volume.[22] However, the very existence of the Internet does not a public sphere make. This study of the current version of electronic public space demonstrates how inadequate it actually is for that purpose.

"Public" Space

So what are the ingredients for such public space? One critical element is the public nature of the space. Unfortunately, too much of what passes for public space today is hardly public. It is either available only to a few, such as private mailing lists or bulletin boards on select, closed spaces, or it is governed by a particular group or individual.

The goal of such spaces is to further the particular creator's agenda, either commercial or policy-oriented. Web sites established by various entities—corporations, associations, groups, public officials, and even candidates—emphasize disseminating the organization's message while slighting or completely avoiding interactivity with site visitors. Interest groups similarly have developed newsgroups or mailing lists. However, these public spaces are either controlled by a single commercial entity or are designed for the self-interest of a narrowly focused group.

Another conception of public space is that provided by government. One might argue that the Web pages of representative bodies, such as the U.S. Senate or a state legislature, constitute public space. But public space is more than governmental space.[23] It encompasses an area not controlled by government. For example, Barber's Civic Communications Cooperative proposes a model close to the British Broadcasting Corporation, that is, funded by government but separate from it.

Various commercial entities such as Microsoft and America Online have sought as well to create electronic public space. However, again the main objective is to further their particular corporate interests. The "public" becomes not the American public but their particular clientele.

The ideal public space would not eliminate commercial interests. Commercial interests could be invited to participate, since they also constitute public voices. But ideal public space would not be dominated by a single commercial entity or any group of related entities, such as a particular industry.

Neither funding nor content of public space should be dominated by these interests. Funding should originate from a large consortium of commercial interests and/or private foundation grants. In sum, ideal public space must be truly public, open to all citizens. Moreover, it must treat them as citizens, not as customers.

Community Membership

The ideal public space requires a sense of community on the part of participants. Currently, online discussants frequently come and go at will with no sense of belonging. In the ideal public space, participants must be required to actually take on membership in the online community.

Moreover, they must be publicly associated with that community or group. Every participant needs to know who other participants are, rather than having a veil of anonymity covering the participants. People must express their opinions openly in public space. The sense of participating in a community should enhance the feeling of acceptance by others who similarly have made a commitment to the group and each of its participants. Those who participate in the group discussion would have to agree to abide by certain community rules. These rules would be designed to foster community interaction and minimize irresponsible behavior such as flaming.

Moreover, individuals ought to be connected to a particular group. By contrast, Usenet allows widespread cross-posting, as mentioned in Chapter 2. In ideal public space, messages would be limited to a single group in order to facilitate conversation within that group. The purpose of inculcating a feeling of belonging would be to create a sense of accountability within the group, which is still another essential ingredient of ideal public space.

Accountability

Stephen Jones has observed that online groups lack a sense of connectedness. Online groups are "not composed of people who are necessarily connected, even by interest, but are groupings of people headed in the same direction, for a time. They may read the same things, occupy the same chat rooms for a time, view the same World Wide Web pages."[24] Jones concludes that community requires "human occupancy, commitment, interaction, and living among and with others."[25]

In ideal public space, accountability would be promoted, not discarded. To begin with, individuals would need to identify themselves by name and location. They also would need to make a commitment to participate in a group for a set period of time. This would include both posters and lurkers, in order to discourage voyeurism. One mechanism to achieve this would be the posting of the full names (not just screen names) of group members alongside the discussion thread so that individuals become aware of everyone else who is part of the conversation—vocal or silent.

That sense of accountability to others in a group might reattach individuals to a sense of community. Regular encouragement of lurkers to participate also would be a feature of ideal public space. More fundamentally, a sense of accountability might facilitate their participation because they feel some stake in the outcome of the discussion. Group members who usually lurk may feel a responsibility to assist in the community's deliberative process in order to reach a resolution that enhances the common good. Participants then would feel an obligation to present information they possess and opinions they hold in order to benefit the whole.[26]

Equality

Online deliberation voices should be equal.[27] For example, they should not be based on the financial worth of the individual. They should not be discriminated according to the type of ideology of the individual. The existence of an individual as a citizen should guarantee that person a voice that can be expressed and will be heard. Online discussion, ideally, offers that type of equality, particularly as Internet use generally reaches a saturation point within the public.

However, the fact that all individuals can participate equally does not mean they actually need to do so. Equality of opportunity for expression is more desirable and attainable than equality of actual expression. Nevertheless, ideal discussion demands the removal of barriers to equality of opportunity in participation, such as exclusion by an elite group or dominance by a single individual, which rob others of the opportunity to participate.[28]

Moreover, the system should take one step beyond merely offering the structural opportunity for involvement. Periodically, the moderator should encourage participation by those who normally are silent in order to ensure that their unique voices are heard in the public deliberative process.[29]

Deliberation

The emphasis of online discussion forums is on self-expression. However, there is increasing doubt about whether such a goal, in and of itself, accomplishes anything. Certainly, such expression is essential to the public deliberative process. Moreover, the climate should be conducive to such expression—that is, people should feel that they can express themselves in a context of listening to and consideration of a variety of viewpoints.

Nevertheless, having expression as the sole goal accomplishes little for a democratic society seeking conflict resolution. The emphasis should be on more than mere expression. According to David Mathews, expression "is all well and good, but if that is all there is in our political conversations, we are in trouble."[30]

In its current manifestation, the failure of electronic political talk to serve democratic society is its failure to move beyond public expression. John Streck notes that the "crucial flaw of cyberspace is that it elevates the right to speak above all others, and all but eliminates the responsibility to listen."[31] Stephen G. Jones adds: "Perhaps it is the case that the Internet allows us to shout more loudly, but whether our fellows listen, beyond the few individuals who may reply, or the occasional lurker, is questionable, and whether our words will make a difference is even more in doubt."[32] Listening is the missing ingredient in current public space. Frances Moore Lappé and Paul Martin DuBois argue that "the first art of democracy is active listening."[33]

Another facet missing from current online political talk is a sense of closure or resolution. One advocate of Usenet has argued that it "provides a forum where there is no ideological closure."[34] Ideological closure may not occur, but perhaps policy closure or the achievement of a consensus on a policy solution, can. Expression and listening plus policy closure are all elements of a deliberative process. Such a process should be part of online political discussion; but clearly it is not.

Ideal public space needs to be a deliberative sphere as well. Individuals should be encouraged to engage in a deliberative process combining elements of political learning and problem solving. Deliberation is not merely an "extra" in a democratic society. It needs to be a fundamental element. Not only does deliberation aid the political system generally, but it also has been found to increase the political sophistication of individuals.[35] Individuals benefit by acquiring increased understanding of political issues and appreciation for issue complexity.

Deliberation in ideal space also would affect the reasons people would participate in online forums. Individuals would realize they are there not merely to express their preferences but also to help facilitate solutions. Such a role conception might alter how people perceive their place in a democratic society. Ralph Ketcham suggests a concept of citizenship where decision making is based on "the idea of a public good" and disinterestedness is promoted.[36] Perhaps online forums as deliberative bodies rather than soapboxes would foster such realization concerning "the idea of a public good."

Deliberation in a public sphere presupposes the existence of certain elements. Some of those elements include learning, public agenda setting, issue focus, a moderating role, and the participation (at least in a listening capacity) of policy makers.

Learning

Deliberation requires openness to learning, particularly from the expressions of others. Benjamin R. Barber argues that "when talk is merely an exchange of fixed opinions and politics is a series of compromises in which positions are arbitrated but never altered, then citizenship is impaired."[37] Ideal public space should promote such willingness. Participants in deliberation should be encouraged to listen and acquire background information about the issues they are discussing.

Moreover, ideal public space must facilitate citizen education as well. One frequent complaint of public officials is the absence of education on the part of individual citizens who voice complaints about policy decisions. The integration of online discussion and online information in a public space can further both activities. The ideal public space would offer places where individuals not only can discuss issues of relevance to them but also educate themselves about those issues. But how would this be done?

One method is the establishment of various public space "topic corners" or "learning corners" where information can be readily obtained on specific issues. Various policy experts may be invited to write short briefing papers on pending policy issues. Representatives of groups could submit succinct position papers explaining their groups' positions on the issues under discussion.

Moreover, access could be made available from such public space corners to other additional sources, such as original documents, for those seeking more information on the issue. These could range from the annual report of a tobacco company to a congressional committee report to the text of the U.S. Constitution. However, the goal would be to maintain individuals on the site rather than leading them off the public space through a maze of links.

Participant usage of learning corners would have short-term and long-term consequences. Individuals would be more likely not only to become generally educated about issues but also to become capable of employing what they have learned in support of subsequent posted arguments. The gains would be in accordance with a study determining that information gathering followed by discussion is better than either of these activities alone.[38]

Public Agenda Setting

Ideal public space must not become the province of elites who dictate public agendas. It must offer participants the opportunity to help set that agenda. Another extreme to avoid is rule by the loudest and most persistent. This means individuals should not be allowed to muscle their way into the conversation and control the group discussion.

But how is it possible to keep the agenda fluid enough to facilitate citizen involvement and allow for new concerns to surface, but not so porous that it can be manipulated by a few? That is the paradox for online agenda setting.

One solution is the usage of a rolling survey of potential issues. Individuals could add policy topics for potential discussion, and the rest of the participants on the space would be invited to vote on which issues would be placed on the space's agenda for creation as a separate group. Majority support (or at least significant minority support) for issue discussion would place the item on the agenda for discussion. Conversely, lack of sufficient interest in a discussion topic would result in elimination of that subject for that particular group. This process would allow individuals the opportunity to attempt to set the agenda. But it also requires a sufficient level of agreement across the group in order for the agenda to be changed to include the new item.

Focus

A common problem with current online discussion is the absence of focus. Newsgroups, chat room, and sometimes even e-mail lists tend to meander across topics. In ideal public space, discussion would need to focus on a specific topic and remain with it until the group votes to change it or it appears that resolution has occurred. Such constancy would encourage the group to stick with a problem until it is resolved and to discourage individuals from using the forum as a mechanism primarily for self-expression rather than deliberation.

This approach assumes that ideal public space would be divided into several topic areas, particularly related to current events or pending policy problems. With such specific jurisdictional areas, groups would attract individuals with concerns for that particular subject.

Inevitably, attempts to move the discussion off the topic will occur, particularly initially, when the concept of focus is still new. As a solution, individuals who seek to veer from the group's topic would be encouraged to participate in another related group or, if none exists, offer the discussion topic as a candidate for the upcoming discussion agenda.

Moderating Role

Still another drawback of current online political talk is the absence of moderators. Some online providers have included group monitors who do discipline individual posters. For example, AOL commonly deletes messages or marks postings with demerits. Other bulletin board administrators, such as those on Yahoo!, also reserve the right to remove postings. Obviously, such disciplining offends many posters.[39] However, these monitors or administrators are generally silent except in the wake of bad behavior. They do not actually lead discussion to fruitful outcomes.

Groups on the ideal public space should be moderated by assigned group chairs. As in other online provider forums, these individuals would be responsible for monitoring the discussion to eliminate those individuals seeking to use the group for other purposes. Also, ad hominem attacks or inflammatory messages would not be allowed.

Admittedly, the concept of moderated discussions raises the specter of censorship, which many discussion group participants argue is a cure worse than the disease. According to one scholar, such moderation "disempowers those whose grievances may be most severe."[40] Yet the benefits of moderation far outweigh the costs. The presence of rules actually ensures that discussion is broad-based, as long as individuals abide by certain standards of civility. One study found that moderated discussions are more civil, with much less flaming.[41] Individuals whose grievances are severe will be allowed, even encouraged, to participate, but will be asked to do so in a mode that invites attention, not summary dismissal. Harris

Breslow argues that public space mediates our behavior by placing rules of conduct on us via social expectations.[42]

Moderation goes beyond that function, however. Moderators will not be mere monitors. They also will carry responsibility for the direction of the discussion, keeping it tied to the topic. This function may require the moderator at times to reformulate issues in order to reach solutions.[43] The moderator then would need to pose questions and raise related topics to stimulate discussion. Simultaneously, the moderator should remind the participants of their goal of achieving problem resolution.

There are clear benefits of moderation for those who participate in online talk. Moderation means the conversation is not dominated by a single individual. Individual participants can feel like they carry equal weight even if they are not aggressive.

Obviously, a related fear would be the power of the chair. The chair's function would not be to dominate the discussion, as is so often true on e-mail lists, but to facilitate it by encouraging participants to become involved in seeking solutions to problems and weighing the consequences of such proposed solutions. It means leading participants to sources where they can gain further information on the topic and then return to the discussion.

Moderators also would be responsible for drawing participants out into the open, particularly those who may feel inhibited. The moderator would need to create a climate within which individuals feel their comments are welcome and the deliberative process is active.

Public Official Role

Public officials rarely actually participate in online discussion. When such participation does occur, it is largely unidirectional: citizens ask questions and policy makers answer. In other settings, it is distinctly private. In other words, policy makers may discuss among themselves on exclusive e-mail lists, but not on lists including ordinary citizens. Deliberation online involving both citizens and policy makers is largely absent from current online political talk.

The absence of public officials from the actual discussion online is not surprising. Obviously most public officials would be disinterested in participating in the chaos that constitutes current forums such as Usenet. They are more likely to enter chat rooms to offer the illusion of conversation. But again the purpose is largely question and answer, rather than public deliberation.

Ideal public space needs to include public officials. Such inclusion should at least include a role for lurkers, which entails listening. Listening would mean they would see citizens at work in a deliberative process and perhaps be influenced by the viewpoints expressed and the solutions offered.

But a more desirable outcome would be the actual participation of public officials. They should express themselves and help work toward deliberative outcomes. For some public officials, such involvement could have the same ameliorating effect as it does on citizens. They, too, may gain greater appreciation for issue complexities and be less prone to be dogmatic. Some also may learn that deliberation may be more appealing to the public than the crystallization of issue stances designed to appeal to extremist or single-issue groups.

Multiple Spaces

Ideal public space is better perceived as ideal public *spaces*. There should be no single central public space. The ideal public space is multiple and diverse. Moreover, it exists on a variety of levels—international, national, regional, and local. In fact, public space may best be implemented at the local level, where issues are proximate and may attract even those who are generally less interested in politics than they are in civics. Community issues—property tax increases, quality of educational services, growth, and so on—are more likely to heighten citizen interest in participation in public space due to their greater effect on individuals in a geographical community.

Who administers these multiple public spaces? Administrators could be local educational institutions, existing nonpartisan groups such as the League of Women Voters, or new nonpartisan organizations specifically designed to further this task.

A Viable Medium

Is this vision of public space possible on the Internet? Absolutely. The medium possesses the potential to serve as such a mechanism. The creation of such electronic public space is achievable if current knowledge about the requirements for public deliberation is applied, and if interests seeking to use public space for narrow policy ends are kept in check.

This is not a proposal for initiatives and referenda, electronically or by other means, as has been suggested by others.[44] Public space would not be a vehicle for actual policy enactment. Nor would it be a mechanism for electing officials and replacing representative government.

Rather, public space might, as one scholar has posited, provide the opportunity for implementing Madisonian democracy. It "might help prevent the 'intemperate and pernicious resolutions, monuments to deficient wisdom,' that Madison thought often characterized the hasty acts of faction-ridden legislatures."[45]

The purpose of ideal public space would be threefold: education of citizens, discussion among citizens and between citizens and policy makers, and deliberation leading to societal problem resolution.

Such space could possess distinct governance advantages. It could offer Americans a place to prepare themselves for approaching policy makers with their issue concerns. It might provide elected officials with insights on public thinking under a deliberative process. It might also enhance respect for politics and the political process as individual citizens and policy makers come together in deliberation to find positive solutions to pressing social problems.

The Future

Benjamin Barber has called for the creation of a "civic Internet," one that fosters civic deliberation and participation instead of being devoted wholly to commercialism.[46] Barber advocates the creation of a national civic forum facilitated by the Internet. He suggests such a forum would allow "citizens to rediscover their civic competence."[47]

The concept is not far from reality. Some groups already are attempting to put such a creation into place. A number of nonprofit organizations now sponsor campaign-related Web sites designed as quasi-public space. During the 2004 election, these included Project Vote Smart and D-Net. News organizations also include sections where voters can obtain information outside of traditional news channels. In addition, many feature chat rooms where questions can be posed to expert guests, or bulletin boards where readers can "talk back" to the news stories.

These offerings have drawbacks. First, they often thrive in electoral periods and become moribund at other times. However, public participation certainly extends beyond electoral periods. Additionally, most current sites emphasize one-way communication—candidate or politician to citizen. However, what is absent, or present only in a limited way, is real interaction. Moreover, such interaction is not likely in the future. Beyond the presence of an e-mail address, the Web sites of candidates in the recent presidential campagns has rarely included interaction with voters. One exception was the "town hall" feature of the Gore campaign site, where questions posed by citizens were answered by the 2000 campaign.[48] Still another was the campaign blog in 2004, when campaigns actually took ideas from supporters.

More interactive online public spaces are being created by nonprofit organizations. Minnesota E-Democracy is a project designed to create public spaces in Minnesota, as well as provide election information for Minnesota citizens.[49] A similar organization exists in Iowa. The Minnesota organization calls itself a "neutral" forum that offers people the opportunity "to float ideas or spread their political spin directly to other citizens." Does that mean that public space in nonelectoral settings, including interaction among citizens, also will evolve? Such emergence may not be natural and may come about only through prompting by various political entities, including government.

Government may need to play a role in ensuring that space remains open for public use and appropriate funding is existent for civic uses. Barber contends that without a government role, the Internet's fate will be the same as that shared by radio, television, and cable—primarily, if not exclusively, commercially driven media.[50] He argues that the Internet can be a beneficial tool for "democracy, civic, culture, and education."[51] Yet those kinds of visions were placed on previous media with mixed success.

The development of ideal public space clearly will require the cooperation of government, commercial, and noncommercial entities. Commercial entities will need to exhibit a public-mindedness that reflects their interest in being citizens much like others. Noncommercial bodies, such as academic institutions and traditional good-government groups, may need to serve as neutral supports for the technological structure.

Finally, government may need to provide funding to enable public space to exist without having to rely heavily on major commercial interests and overcome the temptation to succumb to corporate support in return for corporate roles. Such support should come not only from federal government sources, such as the National Science Foundation, but also from state and local governments.

The creation of ideal public space will require a willingness on the part of all concerned to engage in innovativeness. Therein may be the rub. Technology may not be the major barrier to implementation of public space. The real deterrent may be human attitudes and behavior. Political actors may have to communicate and cooperate in ways that will be new and foreign.

One encumbrance will be unwillingness on the part of public officials to allow individual citizens to interject themselves into the public policy-making process by deliberating on public policy. Some public officials and citizens may hold philosophical objections to the concept of direct democracy implied in ideal public space.

Such an objection is inaccurate. Deliberation is not direct democracy. Individual participants are not making policy. They are interacting with policy makers in the process of policy formulation, but they do not hold responsibility for actually making policy. Voters will still elect representatives who will hold actual policy-making power. None of the outcomes of an online deliberative process would be binding on anyone.

Public officials may not be the only ones lacking confidence in the process. Citizens may not want to participate because they perceive such involvement ultimately to be fruitless. Citizen participation requires a certain level of trust that the process will offer them a voice. Mass media such as radio and television have helped transform citizens into passive entities left primarily with a recipient (or, even worse, spectator) role in American politics. Political communication has featured candidates and public officials transmitting messages to the public—fireside chats, nationally televised addresses, candidate speeches, news conferences, photo opportunities, campaign advertisements, and so on. Given the high levels of public cynicism noted at the beginning of this book, it may take some time to overcome public doubts that citizens actually can be included in the deliberative process.

Citizens may not be willing to invest time in the process. The kind of citizen involvement envisioned by proponents of Internet democracy requires "the necessary leisure on the part of the citizen to devote his or her thoughts and time to public questions."[52] That leisure, although greater than in the past, still is either not actually present or, if present, would not necessarily be filled by political matters.

There is little support for the conclusion that the mere existence of new communications technology will make political activists out of ordinary people.[53] The existence of a seemingly innumerable host of online options, even in electronic discussion forums, makes the choice of political discussion even more unlikely than when media choices were more limited.

The existence of online technology provides the vehicle for inclusion. But the real barrier may be lack of trust on both sides. On one side, given the long dominance of unidirectional technology, the reluctance of public officials to view citizens as more than objects to be manipulated in electoral periods may be a major obstacle. On the citizenry's side, it is the lack of trust in public officials' acceptance of a role for citizens that may hamper citizen utilization of public space. Disappointment and frustration could be the outcome of online interaction as well. In the final analysis, it may be the human barriers to creating ideal public space that are far more formidable than the technological ones.

Appendix: Methodology

Electronic discussion, like other facets of the Internet, can be ephemeral. Messages in chat rooms scroll across the screen and are gone. Newsgroup messages may remain temporarily (perhaps a number of weeks), but not for long periods of time. The exception is the archives kept by some Web sites.

This study, then, deals with a transitory medium. The references to various groups indicate a snapshot in time. If the reader goes to those groups now, the messages will be different and the agendas may have changed considerably.

For example, the comparison between the online discussion community and the general public covered particular periods of time: the surveys of the online discussants and of the general public occurred during the fall of 1998, when the Pew Center posed questions about online discussion, while the comparison of issue agendas of the four Usenet groups and the general public occurred during the fall of 1999.

Content Analysis of Usenet Messages

This study included a content analysis of four Usenet groups. The number of political groups is large. Selecting a small number of groups offers the opportunity to analyze the exchange of messages therein with greater depth. However, such a small sample of groups raises another problem—generalization. It is hard to know whether the discussion of these groups is typical of political discussion groups. That is a question that cannot be answered here. It will come as others conduct similar studies of other groups.

I sought to include representatives of differing types of groups, including the more mainstream as well as the radical fringe, the political left and the political right. The groups selected were alt.politics.radical-left, alt.politics.clinton, alt.politics.usa.republican, and alt.politics.usa.constitution. The first two groups represent the political left, the latter two the political right. The second group is person-oriented and was expected to attract more Usenet participants from the political center-left. The first and fourth represent more extreme political groups: alt.politics.radical-left discusses radical theory, while alt.politics.usa.constitution leans heavily in content toward right-wing agenda items such as high taxes, gun control, or criticism of the Clinton administration. The second and third groups are more moderate in their approach. They tend to attract those closer to the political center—traditional liberals and conservatives.

All posted messages during a one-week period (June 14–20, 1997) were downloaded for each of these groups. The posted messages were identified and coded. This week's worth of message traffic for each group resulted in 1,416 messages coded on alt.politics.usa.republican, 743 on alt.politics.Clinton, 212 on alt.politics.constitution, and 711 on alt.politics.radical-left.

Using a list of "most important issues" created by the Harris Survey, the topics for discussion threads for a six-day period (October 25–30, 1999) for these four groups also were categorized. The number of threads over a one-week period varied from 178 on alt.politics.usa.republican to 10 on alt.politics.usa.constitution. Since there is extensive cross-posting across groups, some of these threads appeared simultaneously on more than one group during this one-week period.

The analysis did not examine the number of messages on each thread. However, they varied widely, from two to twenty. This sample does not include attempted threads, that is, individual posts that were never responded to. It also does not include "announce" posts. The only example of an announce post in this week for these groups was a set of eleven posts containing White House press releases and texts of briefings posted on alt.politics.clinton.

Coding the threads was done by identifying the title, or in the case of a vague title the content of the first message in the thread during the week. Some of these threads had started prior to the week, as indicated by the fact that the first message was a response to a previous message and not the initiation of a thread. In that case, the first message of the week was used.

The Harris Poll was conducted by telephone during the period September 17–21, 1999. It included a national cross section of 1,009 adults. For more details on the poll, see http://www.harrisinteractive.com/harris_poll/ index.asp.

Online Discussant and General Public Surveys

The Pew Research Center for the People and the Press has conducted regular studies of Internet users. However, surveys of online discussants have been rarer. This survey, included questions isolating online discussants, which was invaluable in undertaking this research. The Pew study was conducted between October 26 and December 1, 1998, and involved a nationwide sample of 3,184 adults, eighteen years of age or older. Interviews with an additional oversample of 1,184 adults who use the Internet also were included. In addition, the Pew results include a nationwide sample of 1,201 adults conducted December 9–13, 1998. The Pew study identified individuals who discussed online. The question asked how often the respondent went online to "communicate with other people through online forums, discussion lists, or chat groups."

Another question was used to distinguish between posters and lurkers. The question asked: "Have you ever expressed an opinion about a political or social issue to a bulletin board, on-line newsgroup, or e-mail list?" Since the question does not specifically mention chat rooms, the number of individuals who post consequently may be lower than the actual number.

Comparison with the general public was made through several surveys. The Pew Research Center for the People and the Press conducted a general public survey at the same time as the Internet user study discussed above. In addition, use was made of data obtained by the National Election Studies, Center for Political Studies, University of Michigan. The "NES Guide to Public Opinion and Electoral Behavior" is available at http://www.umich.edu/~nes/nesguide/nesguide.htm. Also, comparison was made with a Gallup Survey conducted on December 27–28, 1998. The survey can be found at Gallup News Service, "Public Trust in Federal Government Remains High," January 8, 1999, at http://www.gallup.com/poll/releases/pr990108.asp.

Notes

Introduction

1. Brad Knickerbocker, "FBI Keeps Eye on Oklahoma City, Waco Anniversary," *Christian Science Monitor*, April 17, 1998, 5.
2. Mike Wilson, "Private Rant, Public Reaction," *St. Petersburg Times*, January 16, 2001, 1D.
3. Maurice Tamman, "Anti-McKinney Spam E-mail May Be a First," *Atlanta Journal-Constitution*, August 23, 2002, 7D.
4. For current Usenet statistics, see Newsadmin.com at http://www.newsadmin.com.
5. For samples, see Elizabeth Weise, "Forget the Net, Usenet Is the Way to Go," *USA Today*, June 16, 1998, 13E; Thomas E. Weber, "On-Line Talk Is Cheap—But It Doesn't Have to Be—How to Find Smart Chat Amid the Noise," *Wall Street Journal*, July 23, 1998, B6; Leslie Gornstein, "The Unsinkable Usenet: The Internet's Answer to the Water Cooler Just Keeps Gabbing Along, Despite a Flood of Junk Commercial Messages," *Orange County Register*, May 3, 1998, K5; and Rob Pegoraro, "Usenet or Lose It: The Global Conversation Piece," *Washington Post*, January 30, 1998, N40.
6. William Wresch, *Disconnected: Haves and Have-Nots in the Information Age* (New Brunswick, N.J.: Rutgers University Press, 1996), 238.
7. Michael Hauben and Ronda Hauben, *Netizens* (Los Alamitos, Calif.: IEEE Computer Society Press, 1997), 9.
8. Mark Harrison, *The Usenet Handbook* (Sebastopol, Calif.: O'Reilly and Associates, 1995), xi.
9. Pew Research Center for the People and the Press, "Internet News Takes Off," June 8, 1998.
10. Lee Sproull and Samer Faraj, "Atheism, Sex, and Databases: The Net as a Social Technology," in Sara Keisler, ed., *Culture of the Internet* (Mahwah, N.J.: Lawrence Erlbaum Associates, 1997), 41; Harley Hahn and Rick Stout, *The Internet Complete Reference* (Berkeley, Calif.: Osborne McGraw-Hill, 1996).
11. Ninth WWW User Survey, Graphic, Visualization, and Usability Center, Georgia Tech University, June 1998; and Public Opinion Online, December 11, 1997.
12. William Wresch, *Disconnected: Haves and Have-nots in the Information Age* (New Brunswick, N.J.: Rutgers University Press, 1996), 237; and Daniel Burstein and David Kline, *Road Warriors: Dreams and Nightmares Along the Information Highway* (New York: Dutton, 1995), 360.
13. Christopher R. Kedzie, "A Brave New World or a New World Order?" in Keisler, ed., *Culture of the Internet*, 223.
14. See Theodore Roszak, *The Cult of Information: A Neo-Luddite Treatise on High Tech, Artificial Intelligence, and the True Art of Thinking* (Berkeley: University of California Press, 1994), xxv–xxvii.
15. Philip E. Ross, "Garbage Recycler," *Forbes*, December 4, 1995, 260.

16. See Anthony Wilhelm, *Democracy in the Digital Age* (New York: Routledge, 2000); Richard Davis, *The Web of Politics: The Internet's Impact on the American Political System* (New York: Oxford University Press, 1999); Thomas W. Benson, "Rhetoric, Civility, and Community: Political Debate on Computer Bulletin Boards," *Communication Quarterly* 44 (1996): 359–78; Jane Siegal et al., "Group Processes in Computer-Mediated Communication," *Organizational Behavior* 37 (1986): 157–87; and Margaret L. McLaughlin et al., "Standards of Conduct on Usenet," in Stephen G. Jones, ed., *Cybersociety: Computer-Mediated Communication and Community* (Thousand Oaks, Calif.: Sage, 1995), 90–111.
17. See Kevin A. Hill and John E. Hughes, *Cyberpolitics: Citizen Activism in the Age of the Internet* (Lanham, Md.: Rowman and Littlefield, 1998), 52–58.

Chapter 1

1. "Final Tabulation shows Almost 105.4 million voters," Dec. 19, 2000 at http: com/2000/ALLPOLITICS/Stories/12/19/election.TURNOUT.ap/
2. Center for Voting and Democracy, "Committee for the Study of the American Electorate Post-Election News Release," November 8, 2002, at http://www.fairvote.org/turnout/csae2002.htm.
3. Federal Election Commission, "National Voter Turnout in Federal Elections: 1960–1996," at www.fec.gov/index.shtml.
4. Virginia Sapiro, Steven J. Rosenstone, and the National Election Studies, *National Election Studies, 2000: Post-Election Study* (data set), produced and distributed by Center for Political Studies, University of Michigan, Ann Arbor, 2001.
5. Ibid.
6. Ibid.
7. See, for example, Daniel Yankelovich, *Coming to Public Judgment: Making Democracy Work in a Complex World* (Syracuse, N.Y.: Syracuse University Press, 1991).
8. Seymour Martin Lipset and William Schneider, *The Confidence Gap: Business, Labor, and Government in the Public Mind* (New York: Free Press, 1983), 4.
9. Speech by Ross Perot at the Reform Party Convention, Long Beach, California, August 11, 1996, at http://usinfo.state.gov/jourals/itps/1096/jpe/pero.htm
10. Speech by Governor George W. Bush, Cedar Rapids, Iowa, June 12, 1999, at http://www.gwu.edu/~action/bushannc.html.
11. Jeffrey C. Goldfarb, *The Cynical Society: The Culture of Politics and the Politics of Culture in American Life* (Chicago: University of Chicago Press, 1991); Donald L. Kanter and Philip H. Mirvis, *The Cynical Americans: Living and Working in an Age of Discontent and Disillusion* (San Francisco: Jossey-Bass, 1989); Michael Lerner, *The Politics of Meaning* (Reading, Mass.: Addison-Wesley, 1996); and Larry J. Sabato, *The Party's Just Begun: Shaping Political Parties for America's Future* (New York: Scott, Foresman, 1988).
12. Ruy A. Teixeira, *The Disappearing American Voter* (Washington, D.C.: Brookings Institution, 1992).
13. Benjamin Barber, *Strong Democracy: Participatory Politics for a New Age* (Berkeley: University of California Press, 1984).
14. Teixeira, *The Disappearing American Voter;* Barber, *Strong Democracy.*
15. Kanter and Mirvis, *The Cynical Americans,* 286.
16. See, for example, Richard Davis and Diana Owen, *New Media and American Politics* (New York: Oxford University Press, 1998).
17. Nina Eliasoph, *Avoiding Politics: How Americans Produce Apathy in Everyday Life* (New York: Cambridge University Press, 1998), 260–61.
18. Benjamin R. Barber, *A Place for Us: How to Make Society Civil and Democracy Strong* (New York: Hill and Wang, 1998), 114–15.
19. See ibid.; and Barber, *Strong Democracy.*
20. Joseph S. Nye Jr., "Introduction: The Decline of Confidence in Government," in Joseph S. Nye Jr. et al., *Why People Don't Trust Government* (Cambridge, Mass.: Harvard University Press, 1997), 18.
21. Stephen G. Jones, "Information, Internet, and Community," in Stephen G. Jones, ed., *Cybersociety 2.0: Revisiting Computer-Mediated Communication and Community* (Thousand Oaks, Calif.: Sage, 1998), 3.

22. For a contrarian view, see Burstein and Kline, *Road Warriors.*
23. Christa Daryl Slaton, *Televote: Expanding Citizen Participation in the Quantum Age* (New York: Praeger, 1992), 205.
24. Anthony Corrado and Charles M. Firestone, eds., *Elections in Cyberspace: Toward a New Era in American Politics* (Washington, D.C.: The Aspen Institute, 1996), 29.
25. Barber, *Strong Democracy,* 274.
26. Ibid.
27. F. Christopher Arterton, *Teledemocracy: Can Technology Protect Democracy* (Newbury Park, Calif.: Sage, 1987); Lawrence Grossman, *The Electronic Republic* (New York: Penguin Books, 1995); and Gary W. Selnow, *Electronic Whistle-Stops: The Impact of the Internet on American Politics* (Westport, CT: Praeger, 1998), 191–203.
28. See, for example, Jacques Ellul, *The Technological Society* (New York: Vintage, 1967); Neil Postman, *Technopoly* (New York: Alfred A. Knopf, 1992); and Robert W. McChesney, *Rich Media Poor Democracy: Communications Politics in Dubious Times* (Champaign: University of Illinois Press, 1999).
29. Douglas Schuler, *New Community Networks: Wired for Change* (New York: ACM Press, 1996), p. 143.
30. Pew Research Center for the People and the Press, "Online Newcomers More Middle-Brow, Less Work-Oriented: The Internet News Audience Goes Ordinary," January 14, 1999, at http://www.people-press.org/reports/display.php3?ReportID=72
31. Still another discussion forum is called a MUD. It is an acronym for "multi-user domains." This model is not included because it is used primarily as a fantasy room. for adventure games. It has not been a significant forum for political discussion.
32. See Catalist, at http://www.lsoft.com/lists/listref.html.
33. Kara L. Robinson, "People Talking to People," *Online* 20 (1996): 26.
34. Marc A. Smith and Peter Kollock, *Communities in Cyberspace* (London: Routledge, 1999), 5.
35. Bill Thompson and Scott Aikens, "If Only Jefferson Had Had E-Mail," *New Statesman,* February 20, 1998, 22.
36. "Talking Online: Chat Groups and Discussion Lists," *Trial* 34 (1998): 91.
37. Kate Wittenberg, "Cutting-edge Scholarship and Electronic Publishing," *The Chronicle of Higher Education,* June 19, 1998, B6.
38. "H-SHEAR Is Here: SHEAR Goes Online," *Journal of the Early Republic* 16 (1996): 107.
39. Richard C. Overbaugh, "Large-Group E-Mail Communication: Management Nightmare and the Listserv Solution," *The Clearing House,* July–August 1998, 355.
40. See HIVline at http://www.hivline.com.
41. Judith S. Donath, "Identity and Deception in the Virtual Community," in Marc A. Smith and Peter Kollock, eds., *Communities in Cyberspace* (London: Routledge, 1999).
42. For a description of the specializations of each of these categories, see Mark Harrison, *The Usenet Handbook* (Sebastopol, Calif.: O'Reilly and Associates, 1995), 14–16.
43. "Master List of Newsgroup Hierarchies," at http://www.magma.ca/~leisen/mlnh/index.html, accessed April 29, 2005.
44. For a discussion of the history of Usenet, see Henry Spencer and David Lawrence, *Managing Usenet* (Sebastopol, Calif.: O'Reilly and Associates, 1998), 406–23; Michael Hauben and Ronda Hauben, *Netizens* (Los Alamitos, Calif.: IEEE Computer Society Press, 1997), 115–20; and Mark Harrison, *The Usenet Handbook* (Sebastopol, Calif.: O'Reilly and Associates, 1995), 6–9.
45. Brendan Kehoe, "Zen and the Art of the Internet: A Beginner's Guide to the Internet," 1st ed., January 1992, at http://www.cs.indiana.edu/docproject/zen/zen-1.0_Toc.htm.
46. Spencer and Lawrence, *Managing Usenet,* 409–10.
47. Lee Sproull and Samer Faraj, "Atheism, Sex, and Databases: The Net as a Social Technology," in Sara Keisler, ed., *Culture of the Internet* (Mahwah, N.J.: Lawrence Erlbaum Associates, 1997), 41.
48. Mark Smith, "Netscan: A Tool for Measuring and Mapping Social Cyberspaces," at http://netscan.research.microsoft.com.
49. Howard Wolinsky, "Where Great or Idle Thoughts Never Die: **Deja News** Archives Millions of Net Messages," *Chicago Sun-Times,* April 2, 1998, 38.
50. See "Google Acquires Usenet Discussion Service and Significant Assets from Deja.com," press release, February 12, 2001, at http://www.google.com/press/pressrel/pressrel48.html;

and note at Google's Usenet Archive, at http://groups.google.com/googlegroups/deja_announcement.html.

51. Hauben and Hauben, *Netizens*, ix and x.
52. Sproull and Faraj, "Atheism, Sex, and Databases," 45–46.
53. Pavlik, *New Media Technology*, 310–11.
54. GVU Sixth WWW User Survey, October/November 1996, at *http://www.gvu.gatech.edu/user_surveys/survey-10-1996*.
55. Peter H. Lewis, "Strangers, Not Their Computers, Build a Network in Time of Grief," *New York Times*, March 8, 1994, A1.
56. See, for example, Evan Schwartz, "Internet Bulletin Boards Create a Sense of Community," in Charles Cozic, ed., *The Information Highway*, (San Diego: Greenhaven Press, 1996), 103–6.
57. Hauben and Hauben, *Netizens*, 3.
58. John M. Streck, "Pulling the Plug on Electronic Town Meetings: Participatory Democracy and the Reality of the Usenet," in Chris Toulouse and Timothy W. Luke, eds., *The Politics of Cyberspace: A New Political Science Reader* (New York: Routledge, 1998), 34–35.
59. Malcolm R. Parks and Kory Floyd, "Making Friends in Cyberspace," *Journal of Communication* 46 (1996): 80–97.
60. Ibid., 94.
61. Mike Snider, "Media Hounded Her, Net's Voices Assert," *USA Today*, September 2, 1997, 1D.
62. Nancy Beym, "The Emergence of On-line Community," in Stephen G. Jones, ed., *Cybersociety 2.0: Revisiting Computer-Mediated Communication and Community* (Thousand Oaks, Calif.: Sage, 1998), 35–68.
63. Donath, "Identity and Deception," 30.
64. Gary Gumpert and Susan Drucker, "The Demise of Privacy in a Private World: From Front Porches to Chat Rooms," *Communication Theory* 8 (1998): 408–25.
65. Ibid., 422.
66. Beym, "The Emergence of On-line Community," 46.
67. Christopher Stoll, *Silicon Snake Oil* (New York: Doubleday, 1995).
68. Ellis Close, "The Trouble with Virtual Grief," *Newsweek*, August 2, 1999, p. 30.
69. Peter H. Lewis, "Strangers, Not Their Computers, Build a Network in Time of Grief," *New York Times*, March 8, 1994, A1.
70. Harriet Wilkins, "Computer Talk: Long-Distance Conversations by Computer," *Written Communication* 8 (1991): 56–78.
71. Stephen G. Jones, "Information, Internet, and Community," in Stephen G. Jones, ed., *Cybersociety 2.0: Revisiting Computer-Mediated Communication and Community* (Thousand Oaks, Calif.: Sage, 1998), 21–30.
72. Pam Belluck, "Stuck on the Web; Symptoms of Internet Addiction," *New York Times*, December 1, 1996, sec. 4, 5; and Nicole Bondi, "Warning: Internet Can be Habit-Forming," *Detroit News*, January 14, 1997, C6. For a contrary view asserting that Internet addiction does not exist, see Steven Levy, "Breathing Is Also Addictive," *Newsweek*, December 30, 1996–January 6, 1997, 52.
73. Bill Gates, *The Road Ahead* (New York: Viking, 1995), 205–11.
74. Parks and Floyd, "Making Friends in Cyberspace."
75. Michael D. Mehta and Dwaine E. Plaza, "Pornography in Cyberspace: An Exploration of What's in Usenet," in Keisler, ed., *Culture of the Internet*, 53–67; and Marty Rimm, "Marketing Pornography on the Information Superhighway: A Survey of 917,410 Images, Descriptions, Short Stories, and Animations Downloaded 8.5 Million Times by Consumers in Over 2000 Cities in 40 Countries, Provinces, and Territories," *Georgetown Law Journal* 83 (1995): 1849–934.
76. Kevin A. Hill and John E. Hughes, "Computer-Mediated Political Communication: The USENET and Political Communities," *Political Communication* 14 (1997): 3–27.
77. "FTC Settles Its First Case of Alleged On-Line Fraud," *Wall Street Journal*, November 17, 1994, A4.
78. Susan Zickmund, "Approaching the Radical Other: The Discursive Culture of Cyberhate," in Stephen G. Jones, ed., *Virtual Culture: Identity and Communication in Cybersociety* (Thousand Oaks, Calif.: Sage, 1997), 185–205.
79. John Kifner and Jo Thomas, "Singular Difficulty in Stopping Terrorism," *New York Times*, January 18, 1998, 23; Burstein and Kline, *Road Warriors*, 111–12.

80. U.S. Congress, House, "A Bill to Prevent and Punish Acts of Terrorism, and for Other Purposes," P.L. 104–132, 104th Cong., 2nd sess., April 24, 1996.
81. Amy Harmon, "As America Online Grows, Charges That Big Brother Is Watching," *New York Times*, January 31, 1999, 1.
82. See, for example, Jeff Frentzen, "Usenet's Underbelly: Where the Wild Users Are," *PC Week*, November 17, 1997, 35.
83. Jerome Curry, "Tapping the Internet's Job Search Resources," *Business Communication Quarterly* 61 (1998): 100.
84. Roberta Furger, "Don't Get Mad, Get Online," *PC World*, October 1997, 37.
85. Philip Elmer-Dewitt, "Welcome to Cyberspace," *Time* special issue on cyberspace, spring 1995, 10.
86. Jim Kerstetter, "Making Usenet Useful," *PC Week*, May 25, 1998, 31.
87. John M. Streck, "Pulling the Plug on Electronic Town Meetings: Participatory Democracy and the Reality of the Usenet," in Chris Toulouse and Timothy W. Luke, eds., *The Politics of Cyberspace: A New Political Science Reader* (New York: Routledge, 1998), 34–35.
88. "The State of 'Electronically Enhanced Democracy': A Survey of the Internet," report prepared by the Walt Whitman Center for the Culture and Politics of Democracy, 1997.
89. Pew Research Center for the People and the Press, "Online Newcomers More Middle-Brow."
90. Thomas W. Benson, "Rhetoric, Civility, and Community: Political Debate on Computer Bulletin Boards," *Communication Quarterly* 44 (1996): 363.
91. Jim Kerstetter, "Making Usenet Useful," *PC Week*, May 25, 1998, 31.
92. Greg R. Notess, "DejaNews and Other Usenet Search Tools," *Online* 22 (1998): 74–78.
93. Charles McGrath, "The Internet's Arrested Development," *New York Times Magazine*, December 8, 1996, 84.
94. Stephen Doheny-Farina, *The Wired Neighborhood* (New Haven: Yale University Press, 1996), 55.
95. Herb Brody, "Wired Science," *Technology Review* 99 (1996): 42–51.
96. Thomas W. Benson, "Rhetoric, Civility, and Community: Political Debate on Computer Bulletin Boards," *Communication Quarterly* 44 (1996): 359–78; and Jane Siegal et al., "Group Processes in Computer-Mediated Communication," *Organizational Behavior* 37 (1986): 157–87.
97. McGrath, "The Internet's Arrested Development," 84.
98. Neil Randall, "Can We Chat?" *PC Magazine*, May 27, 1997, 199.
99. Hiawatha Bray, "Chat Gets Real," *Boston Globe*, January 21, 1999, C1.
100. Sandra Block, "Investors Chat Up Funds on the Net," *USA Today*, July 30, 1999, 3B.
101. See Liszt's IRC Directory, at http://www.liszt.com/chat/report.html.
102. Deleted.
103. Daphne Merkin, "A Fatal Step into Twilight," *U.S. News and World Report*, November 25, 1996, 88–89.
104. Mark Mueller, "FBI's Online Dragnet Zeros In on Sex Predators," *Boston Herald*, March 11, 1998, 1.
105. Deleted.
106. David Whelan, "In a Fog About Blogs," *American Demographics*, July/August 2003, 22–23.
107. Perseus, "The Blogging Iceberg—Of 4.12 Million Hosted Weblogs, Most Little Seen, Quickly Abandoned," October 4, 2003, at http://www.perseus.com/blogsurvey/thebloggingiceberg.html.
108. Ibid.
109. Ibid.
110. Al Gore, "Technology," *Discover*, October 1994, 39.
111. Hans K. Klein, "Grassroots Democracy and the Internet: The Telecommunications Policy Roundtable—Northeast (TPR-NE)," paper presented at the Internet Society 1995 International Networking Conference, Honolulu, Hawaii, June 28–30, 1995. For a copy of the paper, see http://www.isoc.org/hmp/paper/164/txt.paper.txt.
112. Steve Clift, "Democracy Is Online," at http://www.e-democracy.org/do/article.html, and http://www.publicus.net/articles/democracyisonline.html.
113. Hauben and Hauben, *Netizens*, 4.
114. Ibid., 26.
115. Anthony Corrado and Charles M. Firestone, eds., *Elections in Cyberspace: Toward a New Era in American Politics* (Washington, D.C.: Aspen Institute, 1996), 17.

116. Hauben and Hauben, *Netizens*, 243.
117. Ibid., 243–44.
118. William Wresch, *Disconnected: Haves and Have-nots in the Information Age* (New Brunswick, N.J.: Rutgers University Press, 1996).
119. U.S. Department of Commerce, "A Nation Online: How Americans are Expanding Their Use of the Internet," February 2002, at http://www.ntia.doc.gov/ntiahome/dn/html/anationonline2.htm.
120. Hauben and Hauben, *Netizens*, 246–53; Burstein and Kline, *Road Warriors*.
121. Langdon Winner, "Privileged Communications," *Technology Review*, May/June 1995, 70.
122. Hauben and Hauben, *Netizens*, 319.
123. Burstein and Kline, *Road Warriors*, 337–60.
124. Barber, *A Place for Us*, 83.
125. Al Gore, "Technology," *Discover*, October 1994, 40.
126. For an example, see H.R. 4324, 105th Congress, 2nd Session.
127. U.S. Department of Education, "Internet Access in U.S. Public Schools and Classrooms: 1994–2001," at http://nces.ed.gov/pubs2002/internet.
128. Kedzie, "A Brave New World or a New World Order?" 227–29.
129. Gates, *The Road Ahead*, 256–57.
130. Ralph Ketcham, *Individualism and Public Life* (New York: Basil Blackwell, 1987), 134–219; Barber, *A Place for Us*; and "The State of 'Electronically Enhanced Democracy.'"
131. See, for example, David Mathews, *Politics for People: Finding a Responsible Voice* (Urbana: University of Illinois Press, 1994); James S. Fishkin, *The Voice of the People: Public Opinion and Democracy* (New Haven: Yale University Press, 1995); Daniel Yankelovich, *Coming to Public Judgment: Making Democracy Work in a Complex World* (Syracuse, N.Y.: Syracuse University Press, 1991); James S. Fishkin, *Democracy and Deliberation: New Directions for Democratic Reform* (New Haven: Yale University Press, 1991); and Barber, *Strong Democracy*.
132. Fishkin, *The Voice of the People*; Fishkin, *Democracy and Deliberation*.
133. For more discussion of the concept of public sphere, see Jürgen Habermas, *The Structural Transformation of the Public Sphere* (Cambridge, MA: MIT Press, 1989).
134. "The State of 'Electronically Enhanced Democracy.'"
135. Pew Research Center for the People and the Press, "Online Newcomers More Middle-Brow."
136. For samples of this argument, see Robert McChesney, "The Internet and U.S. Communication Policy-Making in Historical and Critical Perspective," *Journal of Communication* 46 (1996): 98–124; and Burstein and Kline, *Road Warriors*.
137. John V. Pavlik, *New Media Technology: Cultural and Commercial Perspectives* (Boston: Allyn and Bacon, 1996), 389–90.
138. Gladys D. Ganley, "Power to the People Via Personal Electronic Media," *The Washington Quarterly*, Spring 1991, 20.
139. Howard Fineman, "Who Needs Washington?" *Newsweek*, January 27, 1997, 50.
140. Hauben and Hauben, *Netizens*, 243.
141. Elmer-Dewitt, "Welcome to Cyberspace," 10.
142. Hauben and Hauben, *Netizens*, 225.
143. Ibid., 227.
144. See http://www.americanpressinstitute.org.
145. Guy Berger, "The Internet: A Goldmine for Editors and Journalists," presented to the World Editors Forum, May 1996, at http://www.ru.ac.za/goldmine/gold.htm.
146. Richard Davis, *The Web of Politics: The Internet's Impact on the American Political System* (New York: Oxford University Press, 1999), p. 500.
147. Berger, "The Internet: A Goldmine for Editors and Journalists."
148. Joel Garreau, "A Shaken Global Village on the Internet," *Washington Post*, September 12, 2001, C01.
149. Amy Harmon, "A Day of Terror: The Talk Online; Web Offers Both News and Comfort," *New York Times*, September 12, 2001, A25.
150. William Drozdiak, "World Leaders, Citizens Send Condemnations and Sympathy," *Washington Post*, September 12, 2001, A24; and Richard Boudreaux, "Critics of the U.S. See the Attacks as a Lesson to Temper the Arrogance and Double Standards of a Relatively Young Global Leader," *Los Angeles Times*, September 13, 2001, A12.

151. See http://www.e-democracy.org/mn-politics/explain.html.

152. Heidi Anderson, TK.

153. Whit Andrews, "Surveillance in Cyberspace," *American Journalism Review,* March 1996, 13.

154. For more discussion of presidential campaign use of e-mail and online discussion, see Bruce Bimber and Richard Davis, *Campaigning Online* (New York: Oxford University Press, 2003).

155. Pew Research Center for the People and the Press, "Cable and Internet Loom Large in Fragmented Political News Universe, Perceptions of Partisan Bias Seen as Growing, Especially by Democrats," January 11, 2004, at http://people-press.org/reports.

156. During the 2004 presidential campaign, meet-up numbers for candidates were available on http://www.meetup.com.

157. Matea Gold, "Where Political Influence Is Only a Keyboard Away," *Los Angeles Times,* December 21, 2003, A41.

158. Bimber and Davis, *Campaigning Online.*

159. Alison Mitchell, "On Patients' Bill, Republicans Defeat Democrats' Provisions," *New York Times,* July 14, 1999, A16.

160. Mark Sappenfield "More Politicians Write Blogs to Bypass Mainstream Media," *Christian Science Monitor,* March 24, 2005, p. 2.

161. Deleted.

162. Deleted.

163. Deleted.

164. "Uncle Sam's Newsgroups," *Government Executive,* August 1997, 12.

165. "Cyber-activism," *Audubon,* March/April 1999, 104; For a current list of their lists, see http://www.audubon.org/nas/contact.html.

166. Peter J. Carnevale and Tahira M. Probst, "Conflict on the Internet," in Keisler, ed., *Culture of the Internet,* 241–43; and Christine Ogan, "List Server Communication During the Gulf War: What Kind of Medium Is the Electronic Bulletin Board?" *Journal of Broadcasting and Electronic Media* 37 (1993): 177–96.

167. Gladys D. Ganley, "Power to the People Via Personal Electronic Media," *Washington Quarterly,* spring 1991, 10–12; and Carnevale and Probst, "Conflict on the Internet."

168. David L. Marcus, "Indonesia Revolt Was Net Driven," in Gray Young, ed., *The Internet* (New York: H. W. Wilson Company, 1998), 109–11.

169. Alice A. Love, "The Age of Cyberlobbying: 'Electronic Advocacy' Field About to Launch Hill Lobbying Revolution," *Roll Call,* March 13, 1995.

170. Quoted in Bart Ziegler and Jared Sandberg, "On-line Snits Fomenting Public Storms," *Wall Street Journal,* December 23, 1994, B1.

171. *The Federalist Papers* (New York: New American Library, 1961).

172. Richard Fenno, *Home Style: House Members in Their Districts* (New York: Addison-Wesley, 1978), 141.

173. Marie Collins Swabey, "The Representative Sample," in Hannah Pitkin, ed., *Representation* (New York: Atherton Press, 1969), 90.

174. See, for example, Henry E. Brady and Gary R. Orren, "Polling Pitfalls: Sources of Error in Public Opinion Surveys," in Thomas E. Mann and Gary R. Orren, *Media Polls in American Politics* (Washington, D.C.: Brookings Institution, 1992), 55–94.

175. See, for example, John W. Kingdon, *Congressmen's Voting Decisions,* 3rd ed. (New York: Harper and Row, 1989); and Aage R. Clausen, *How Congressmen Decide* (New York: St. Martin's Press, 1973).

176. Harold Gosnell, "Pleasing the Constituents," in Pitkin, ed., *Representation,* 111.

177. See J. Roland Pennock and John W. Chapman, eds., *Representation* (New York: Atherton Press, 1968; Pitkin, ed., *Representation,* and Hannah Pitkin, comp., *The Concept of Representation* (Berkeley: University of California Press, 1972).

178. Pitkin, ed., *Representation,* 20–21.

179. See Ross J. S. Hoffman and Paul Levack, *Burke's Politics: Selected Writings and Speeches of Edmund Burke on Reform, Revolution, and War* (New York: Knopf, 1949).

180. Pitkin, comp., *The Concept of Representation,* 60.

Chapter 2

1. From talk.politics.misc on October 26, 2002.
2. Kevin A. Hill and John E. Hughes, *Cyberpolitics: Citizen Activism in the Age of the Internet* (Lanham, Md.: Rowman and Littlefield, 1998), 48.
3. NewsAdmin.Com, at http://www.newsadmin.com.
4. Kevin A. Hill and John E. Hughes, "Computer-Mediated Political Communication: The USENET and Political Communities," *Political Communication* 14 (March 1997): 3–27.
5. See list description at http://www.dir.groups.yahoo.com/dir/government_politics.
6. Mark Harrison, *The Usenet Handbook: A User's Guide to Netnews* (Sebastopol, Calif.: O'Reilly & Associates, 1995), 6–7.
7. Michael Hauben and Ronda Hauben, *Netizens: On the History and Impact of Usenet and the Internet* (Los Alamitos, Cal: IEEE Computer Society Press, 1997), 191.
8. Hill and Hughes, *Cyberpolitics*, 54–55.
9. Hill and Hughes, "Computer-Mediated Political Communication."
10. "The TTLB Blogosphere Ecosystem," at http://www.truthlaidbear.com/ecosystem.php.
11. "Site Traffic," at http://www.andrewsullivan.com/info.php?artnum=000stats.
12. Jennifer Peter, "Dems Invite Bloggers to Cover Convention," *USA Today*, June 2, 2004, at http://www.usatoday.com; and Joanna Weiss, "Blogs Colliding with Traditional Media; Convention Credentials Expected for Web Logs," *Boston Globe*, May 10, 2004, at http://www.boston.com.
13. Kathy Kiely, "Freewriting 'Bloggers' Are Rewriting the Rules of Journalism," *USA Today*, December 30, 2003, p. A1, at http://www.usatoday.com/tech/news/2003-12-30-blogging-usat_x.htm.
14. Mark Glaser, "Trent Lott Gets Bloggered," *USC Annenberg Online Journalism Review*, December 17, 2002, at http://www.ojr.org.
15. Noah Schachtman, "Blogs Make the Headlines," *Wired*, December 23, 2002, at http://www.wired.com.
16. Margaret L. McLaughlin et al., "Standards of Conduct on Usenet," in Stephen G. Jones, eds., *Cybersociety: Computer-Mediated Communication and Community* (Thousand Oaks, Calif.: Sage, 1995), 102.
17. Lee Sproull and Samer Faraj, "Atheism, Sex, and Databases: The Net as a Social Technology," in Sara Keisler, ed., *Culture of the Internet* (Mahwah, N.J.: Lawrence Erlbaum Associates, 1997), 44.
18. Netscan, "News Group Report—alt.politics.radical-left," at http://netscan.research.microsoft.com/reportcard.asp?timespan=m&searchdate=12/31/2003&NGID=12128&searchfor=alt.politics.radical-left.
19. Jonathan Vankin and John Whalen, "How a Quack Becomes a Canard," *New York Times Magazine*, November 17, 1996, 56–57. See also Matthew L. Wald, "Cyber-Mice That Roar, Implausibly," *New York Times*, November 10, 1996, 5.
20. Harriet Wilkins, "Computer Talk: Long-Distance Conversations by Computer," *Written Communication* 8 (1991): 56–78.
21. Christine Ogan, "Listserver Communication During the Gulf War: What Kind of Medium Is the Electronic Bulletin Board?" *Journal of Broadcasting and Electronic Media* 37 (1993): 177–96.
22. Hill and Hughes, *Cyberpolitics*, 56–57.
23. Sproull and Faraj, *Atheism, Sex, and Databases*, 44; and Hill and Hughes, *Cyberpolitics*, 56–57.
24. Amy Harmon, "The American Way of Spam," *New York Times*, May 7, 1998, G1.
25. Netscan, at http://netscan.research.microsoft.com.
26. Daniel Burston and David Kline, *Road Warriors: Dreams and Nightmares Along the Information Highway* (New York: Dutton, 1995), 115.
27. McLaughlin et al., "Standards of Conduct on Usenet," 90–111.
28. Jeffrey M. Taylor, "Liability of Usenet Moderators for Defamation Published by Others: Flinging the Law of Defamation into Cyberspace," *Florida Law Review* 47 (April 1995): 247–86.
29. Nancy Beym, "The Emergence of On-line Community," in Stephen G. Jones, ed., *Cybersociety 2.0: Revisiting Computer-Mediated Communication and Community* (Thousand Oaks, Calif.: Sage, 1998), 56.

30. Judith S. Donath, "Identity and Deception in the Virtual Community," in Marc A. Smith and Peter Kollock, eds., *Communities in Cyberspace* (London: Routledge, 1999), 31.
31. Ogan, "Listserver Communication During the Gulf War."
32. John M. Streck, "Pulling the Plug on Electronic Town Meetings: Participatory Democracy and the Reality of the Usenet," in Chris Toulouse and Timothy W. Luke, eds., *The Politics of Cyberspace: A New Political Science Reader* (New York: Routledge, 1998), 18–47.
33. Charles S. White, "Citizen Participation and the Internet: Prospects for Civic Deliberation in the Information Age," *Social Studies*, January/February 1997, 27.
34. Theodore Roszak, *The Cult of Information: A Neo-Luddite Treatise on High Tech, Artificial Intelligence, and the True Art of Thinking* (Berkeley: University of California Press, 1994), xxvii.
35. White, "Citizen Participation," 28.

Chapter 3

1. The data on Internet users—both online discussants and others—is drawn from a survey conducted by the Pew Research Center. For more information on the survey, see Pew Research Center for the People and the Press, "Online Newcomers More Middle-Brow, Less Work-Oriented: The Internet News Audience Goes Ordinary," January 14, 1999, at http://www.people-press.org/reports/display.php3?ReportID=72.
2. Thomas E. Miller, "Segmenting the Internet," *American Demographics*, July 1996, 48–52.
3. Victor Savicki et al., "Gender Language Style in Group Composition in Internet Discussion Groups," *Journal of Computer-Mediated Communication*, at http://www.ascusc.org/jcmc/vol2/issue3/.
4. Victor Savicki et al., "Gender, Group Composition and Task Type in Small Task Groups Using Computer Mediated Communication," *Computers in Human Behavior.* 12 (1996): 209–24.
5. Michael Hauben and Ronda Hauben, *Netizens* (Los Alamitos, Calif.: IEEE Computer Society Press, 1997), 224–27.
6. Quoted in ibid., 225.
7. Evan Schwartz, "Internet Bulletin Boards Create a Sense of Community," in Charles Cozic, ed., *The Information Highway* (San Diego: Greenhaven Press, 1996), 102.

Chapter 4

1. Jane Manning, William Scherlis, Sara Kiesler, Robert Kraut, and Tridas Mukhopadhyay, "Erotica on the Internet: Early Evidence From the HomeNet Trial," in Sara Kiesler, ed., *Culture of the Internet* (Mahwah, N.J.: Lawrence Erlbaum Associates, 1997), 68–69.
2. Christine Ogan, "Listserver Communication During the Gulf War: What Kind of Medium Is the Electronic Bulletin Board?" *Journal of Broadcasting and Electronic Media* 37 (1993): 177–96.

Chapter 5

1. For example, see Ruy A. Teixeira, *The Disappearing American Voter* (Washington, D.C.: Brookings Institution, 1992), 51.
2. Richard M. Scammon, Alice V. McGillivray, and Rhodes Cook, *America Votes 23: A Handbook of Contemporary American Election Statistics* (Washington, D.C.: CQ Press, 1998).

Chapter 6

1. Nina Eliasoph, *Avoiding Politics* (New York: Cambridge University Press, 1998), 5.
2. "Editorial: Virtual Democracy," *Harvard International Journal of Press/Politics* 3 (1998): 1–4.
3. John Gastil, *Democracy in Small Groups: Participation, Decision Making, and Communication* (Philadelphia: New Society Publishers, 1993), 133–34.
4. David P. Thelen, *Becoming Citizens in the Age of Television: How Americans Challenged the Media and Seized Political Initiative During the Iran-Contra Debate* (Chicago: University of Chicago Press, 1996), 177–92.

5. Putnam, "Bowling Alone: America's Declining Social Capital," *Journ. of Dem.* (JAN, 1995): 76.
6. Amy Harmon, "As America Online Grows, Charges That Big Brother Is Watching," *New York Times*, January 31, 1999, 1.
7. Ananda Mitra, "Virtual Commonality: Looking for India on the Internet," in Stephen G. Jones, ed., *Virtual Culture: Identity and Communication in Cybersociety* (Thousand Oaks, Calif.: Sage, 1997), 66.
8. Jennifer Stromer-Galley, "The Diversity of Political Conversation Online: Users' Perspectives," at http://baserv.vei.kvn.nl/~jankow/euricom/papers/stromer-galley.pdf.
9. See Cass Sunstein, *Republic.com* (Princeton, N.J.: Princeton University Press, 2001).
10. John M. Streck, "Pulling the Plug on Electronic Town Meetings: Participatory Democracy and the Reality of the Usenet," in Chris Toulouse and Timothy W. Luke, eds., *The Politics of Cyberspace: A New Political Science Reader* (New York: Routledge, 1998), 45.
11. Kate Maddox, "Talkway Signs Up 1st Advertisers: Books, Music, Peripherals and Coffee Pitched to Usenet Newsgroups," *Advertising Age*, June 8, 1998, 36; Jim Kerstetter, "Making Usenet Useful," *PC Week*, May 25, 1998, 31; and Susan Kuchinskas, "Spreading the Usenet: SuperNews Repositions," *Brandweek*, December 7, 1998, 36.
12. Maddox, "Talkway Signs Up 1st Advertisers," 36.
13. Jane Siegal et al., "Group Processes in Computer-Mediated Communication," *Organizational Behavior and Human Decision Processes* 37 (1986): 157–87; and Sara Keisler and Lee Sproull, "Group Decision Making and Communication Technology," *Organizational Behavior and Human Decision Processes* 52 (1992): 96–123.
14. Charles S. White, "Citizen Participation and the Internet: Prospects for Civic Deliberation in the Information Age," *Social Studies*, January/February 1997, 27.
15. Jürgen Habermas, *The Structural Transformation of the Public Sphere* (Cambridge, MA: MIT Press, 1989), 26.
16. Eliasoph, *Avoiding Politics*, 11.
17. Habermas, *The Structural Transformation of the Public Sphere*. See also Terry Eagleton, *The Function of Criticism* (London: Verso, 1984).
18. Habermas, *The Structural Transformation of the Public Sphere*, 158.
19. Ibid., 226.
20. Eliasoph, *Avoiding Politics*, 13.
21. Benjamin R. Barber, *Strong Democracy: Participatory Politics for a New Age* (Berkeley, Calif.: University of California Press, 1984), 277–80.
22. For example, see ibid., 267–311; Juliet Roper, "New Zealand Political Parties Online: The World Wide Web as a Tool for Democratization or for Political Marketing?" in Toulouse and Luke, eds., *The Politics of Cyberspace*, 69–83.
23. Habermas, *The Structural Transformation of the Public Sphere*, 2.
24. Stephen G. Jones, "The Internet and Its Social Landscape," in Jones, ed., *Virtual Culture*, 17.
25. Ibid., 16.
26. John Gastil, *Democracy in Small Groups: Participation, Decision Making, and Communication* (Philadelphia: New Society Publishers, 1993), 27–28.
27. Eliasoph, *Avoiding Politics*, 11.
28. Gastil, *Democracy in Small Groups*, 24–25.
29. Ibid.
30. David Mathews, *Politics for People: Finding a Responsible Voice* (Urbana: University of Illinois Press, 1994), 112.
31. Streck, "Pulling the Plug on Electronic Town Meetings," 46.
32. Jones, "The Internet and Its Social Landscape," 30.
33. Francis Moore Lappé and Paul Martin DuBois, "Power in a Living Democracy," *Creation Spirituality*, September/October 1992, 42. Quoted in Gastil, *Democracy in Small Groups*, 31.
34. Mitra, "Virtual Commonality," 74.
35. John Gastil and James Dillard, "Increasing Political Sophistication Through Public Deliberation," *Political Communication* 16 (1999): 3–23.
36. Ralph Ketcham, *Individualism and Public Life* (New York: Basil Blackwell, 1987), 212.
37. Benjamin R. Barber, *A Place for Us: How to Make Society Civil and Democracy Strong* (New York: Hill and Wang, 1998), 118–19.

38. "The State of 'Electronically Enhanced Democracy': A Survey of the Internet," report prepared by the Walt Whitman Center for the Culture and Politics of Democracy, 1997.

39. Harmon, "As America Online Grows," 1.

40. Thomas W. Benson, "Rhetoric, Civility, and Community: Political Debate on Computer Bulletin Boards," *Communication Quarterly* 44 (1996): 361.

41. "The State of 'Electronically Enhanced Democracy.'"

42. Harris Breslow, "Civil Society, Political Economy, and the Internet," in Jones, ed., *Virtual Culture*, 236–57.

43. Gastil, *Democracy in Small Groups*, 27.

44. Barber, *Strong Democracy*, 281–90.

45. Ralph Ketcham, *Individualism and Public Life* (New York: Basil Blackwell, 1987), 207.

46. Barber, *A Place for Us*, 75.

47. Ibid., 89.

48. See Bruce Bimber and Richard Davis, *Campaigning Online* (New York: Oxford University Press, 2003).

49. See Minnesota E-Democracy at http://www.e-democracy.org.

50. Barber, *A Place for Us*, 81–83.

51. Ibid., 80.

52. Simon Sterne, "The Representational Likeness," in Hannah Pitkin, ed., *Representation* (New York: Atherton Press, 1969), 75.

53. F. Christopher Arterton, *Teledemocracy: Can Technology Protect Democracy* (Newbury Park, Calif.: Sage, 1987); and Richard Davis, *The Web of Politics: The Internet's Impact on the American Political System* (New York: Oxford University Press, 1999).

Index

Printed and bound by CPI Group (UK) Ltd, Croydon, CR0 4YY

01/11/2024

01782631-0001

"For years now, civic idealists have touted the internet as a great place to conduct discussions about public affairs. Richard Davis advises us that, from a political science perspective, it is just as important to look at who is talking politics on the Internet as it is to explain how electronic discussions occur. Casting a keen eye on both survey data and online content, Davis argues convincingly that chat rooms and other internet forums cannot yet be regarded as sufficiently representative of public opinion."

—MICHAEL CORNFIELD, Senior Research Consultant, Pew Internet & American Life Project, and author of *Politics Moves Online: Campaigning and the Internet*

"Discussion forums, such as newsgroups, chatrooms, and blogs, are a new force in American politics. Richard Davis rejects the idea that they contribute to direct democracy due to inequalities of access and the fragmented nature of political discussion on them, however. He questions whether they can facilitate true public deliberation, which is central to the revival of participatory democracy, and he argues that citizens should be wary of claims that technology-based processes can resolve issues which should instead be solved by human beings. Discussion forums are, however, serving an important function for political activists and the news media. Davis' timely summation of central issues in the field will be of interest to specialists and citizens alike."

—MONTAGUE KERN, Rutgers University, and co-editor of *Framing Terrorism: The News Media, the Government and the Public*

Online political discussion has been touted by some as a new tool for deliberative or even direct democracy. In **Politics Online** Richard Davis argues that, to the contrary, online forums in their current form lack the representative qualities essential to serve as gauges of public opinion. The author provides a thorough analysis detailing the political attitudes, behavior, and demographic nature of the electronic discussion community as it contrasts with the general public. Basing his findings on an original study including content analysis of discussion groups' messages and surveys of online discussion posters and subscribers, Davis demonstrates that the online discussion community does not mirror the general public it ostensibly represents, and the online environment for participation does not at present foster healthy public discourse. In short, Davis argues, the Internet is not the panacea it is envisioned to be for our democratic ills.

Politics Online is essential reading for those interested —both advocates and skeptics alike— in the democratic potential of the Internet.

RICHARD DAVIS is Professor of Political Science at Brigham Young University. He is the author of *Campaigning Online* (with Bruce Bimber), *The Web of Politics*, and *New Media and American Politics* (with Diana Owen).

ISBN 978-0-415-95193-7

9 780415 951937

Routledge
Taylor & Francis Group